It's Center Time!

by
Marilee Whiting Woodfield

Carson-Dellosa Publishing Company, Inc.
Greensboro, North Carolina

Dedication
to Kira, Tyler, Dan, and Nate

Credits
Editor: Ashley Anderson
Layout Design: Van Harris and Mark Conrad
Inside Illustrations: Janet Armbrust
Cover Design: Peggy Jackson
Cover Illustrations: Dan Sharp

ISBN 1-59441-953-1

Table of Contents

Introduction

Learning centers are an important part of early childhood classrooms because they give students opportunities to develop social skills and learn about classroom themes through self-directed, hands-on experiences. Successful centers require planning and preparation. That's why *It's Center Time!* includes instructions, suggested supply lists, and helpful tips for setting up 14 learning centers, as well as over 150 themed activities to use in those centers. And, each themed activity is conveniently marked with the corresponding center's icon. So, if you need an activity to use in a specific center, look for the corresponding icon within the chapters of themed activities or turn to the Index of Center Activities (pages 79–80) for a list of all of the activities organized by center. Some of the activities are marked with more than one icon because they can be used in more than one type of center.

Each themed chapter contains a variety of activity ideas. You will not find an activity for all 14 centers included in each themed chapter, but you will find activities for the most relevant centers. Additionally, each themed chapter contains suggested books for expanding the classroom library and encouraging independent reading. *It's Center Time!* is a wonderful time-saver and aid for planning a well-rounded center curriculum.

Following are general tips to keep in mind as you create learning centers in the classroom:

❀ ***Plan centers that are student directed.***
   A student should be able to step into the center and begin his play experience without having to retrieve supplies and with little or no instruction or outside involvement.

❀ ***Allow for multiple outcomes.***
   Often the best centers are those that are open-ended; students direct where and when the play begins and stops.

❀ ***Establish and enforce consistent rules.***
   Develop classroom rules that are relevant for all centers, as well as separate rules for each individual center as needed.

❀ ***Offer choices.***
   Encourage students to spend time at each center but allow for individual preferences. Limit the number of centers offered at one time. Too many choices can be overwhelming.

❀ ***Decide how many students can visit each center at one time.***
   This will help with classroom management, and everyone will have more fun.

❀ ***Present each center to the class.***
   Show and demonstrate items in the centers so that there is no confusion about acceptable and unacceptable behavior.

❀ ***Provide opportunities for students to interact with each other.***
   This will help them learn and practice social skills, such as cooperation, negotiation, and sharing.

Setting Up the Centers

Art Center...

The purpose of the art center is to give students an opportunity to create with minimal boundaries while exploring different art mediums. Not only will students have opportunities for creativity and self-expression, they will also gain fine motor skills, such as dexterity, hand strength, and hand-eye coordination as they investigate colors, textures, and cause and effect concepts.

Some Suggested Supplies:
* drop cloths or tarps
* newspaper
* pencils
* chalk
* chenille stems
* paints (tempera, watercolor, etc.)
* paper (construction paper, wallpaper, craft paper, copy paper, bulletin board paper, etc.)
* collage materials (buttons, sequins, dried beans, uncooked pasta, etc.)
* drying rack or table
* paint smocks
* crayons
* scissors
* craft pom-poms
* clothespins
* stamps
* markers
* glue and glue sticks
* felt
* paintbrushes (various sizes)
* easels
* ink pads
* feathers
* craft sticks
* yarn

Caution: Before completing any feather activity, inquire about students' allergies.

Center Setup Tips:
* Set up the art center close to the bathroom or another source of water for quick and easy cleanup.
* Make sure the art center is in an undisturbed location so that other students will be less likely to accidentally come into contact with or spill materials as they walk by.
* Place a large tarp or drop cloth on the floor to catch spills.
* Cover the table with newspaper or a plastic tablecloth.
* Provide paint smocks or large T-shirts to keep clothes clean.

Sample Center Activities

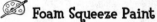 Foam Squeeze Paint
Supplies: liquid tempera paint; shaving cream foam (not gel); empty, clean, plastic squeeze bottles; construction paper

Setup: Pour approximately 2 oz. (59 mL) of liquid tempera paint into a clean plastic squeeze bottle, such as an empty ketchup or mustard bottle. Add approximately 6 oz. (177 mL) of shaving cream foam. Seal the bottle tightly and shake well. Label the bottle with the color of its contents. Repeat to create several different colors.

Directions: Encourage students to squeeze the foam paint onto construction paper to create their own designs or drawings. Place the artwork on a separate table until it is dry.

Textured Easel Painting
Supplies: tempera paint, textured substances (rice, sand, cornstarch, etc.), paper, paintbrushes

Setup: Prepare three different colors of paint, each in a separate container. Stir a textured substance into each container of paint.

Directions: Allow students to experiment with the different textured paints as they create at the easel. While they are painting, engage them in conversation about the textures, discussing the similarities and differences, their favorites and least favorites, etc.

Extension: Extend the activity by allowing students to choose and mix their own paints and textures.

Variation: Provide a sensory experience by allowing students to finger paint with the textured paints.

Blocks Center . . . .

The purpose of the blocks center is to allow students to build and create structures using blocks. While they are building, they learn about shapes, spatial relationships, gravity, and using their imaginations to create and explore. Students also learn to compare sizes, classify blocks by different characteristics, and develop small motor skills.

Some Suggested Supplies:
blocks in a variety of sizes, shapes, and textures, including:
* wood blocks
* foam blocks
* plastic interlocking blocks
* cardboard bricks
* shoe boxes with the lids taped in place
* small accessories, such as toy cars, trucks, road signs, trees, bushes, and plastic animals and figurines

Caution: Some small objects may present choking hazards and are not appropriate for children under age three.

Center Setup Tips:
* Provide bins and shelves for storage. Store each type of block in a separate bin.
* Label each bin and shelf with the name and a picture of the contents for easy cleanup and organization.
* Store large blocks so that each shape has its own shelf space. Then, students won't need to empty an entire bin to find one specific block.
* Providing objects other than blocks, such as small plastic animals, cars, trucks, etc., adds another dimension of interest to the blocks center.

Sample Center Activities

Higher & Higher
Supplies: variety of blocks
Setup: Place the blocks in the blocks center.
Directions: Tell students to practice stacking the blocks as high as possible. As they add to the tower, have them count the number of blocks aloud. Then, instruct students to try stacking blocks in different groups and shapes. For example, encourage students to make a higher stack of blocks built in the shape of a pyramid or in sets of two or three blocks.

Extension: Have each student work with a partner. To take a turn, each player rolls a fair number cube to see how many blocks to add to the tower. For example, if player one rolls a 3, she adds three blocks to the tower. Then, if player two rolls a 5, he adds five blocks to the tower. Students should continue rolling and stacking until the tower topples. Remind them to count the blocks aloud as they add to the tower.

Can You Do This?
Supplies: variety of blocks, "Can You Do This?" binder
Setup: Place the blocks in the blocks center.
Directions: Allow each student (or pair of students) to use the blocks to build a structure without direction from you. Then, take pictures of the creations and place the developed photos inside photo protectors in a binder titled "Can You Do This?" Occasionally, place the binder in the blocks center and let students try to reconstruct the structures by using the pictures for reference.

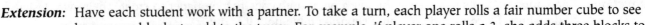

🎭 Dramatic Play Center

Dramatic play gives students opportunities to explore events or thoughts in an imaginative way. It allows students to indulge in self-awareness and conceptual exploration. Dramatic play opportunities also allow for the development of creativity, cooperation, imagination, and problem solving skills.

Some Suggested Supplies:

- ✿ clothes
- ✿ mirror
- ✿ puppet theater

- ✿ costumes
- ✿ props
- ✿ puppets and stuffed animals

- ✿ accessories
- ✿ empty, clean product cartons

Center Setup Tips:

- ✿ Provide a wide assortment of costumes and props. Keep them in large storage bins or use hooks or hangers to keep things organized.
- ✿ Provide chairs for the audience if a dramatic play activity is set up as a performance.
- ✿ Encourage students to create additional roles and include classmates in their play.
- ✿ Allow students to create freely without restrictions.

Sample Center Activities

🎭 Ice Cream Shop

Supplies: construction paper "scoops of ice cream"; empty, clean ice cream cartons with lids; empty, clean plastic bottles and containers for "syrups" and "toppings"; ice cream scoops; bowls; cups; spoons; hats and aprons for workers; tables and chairs for patrons; toy cash register and money manipulatives

Setup: Provide a counter area for workers and a table and chairs for patrons. Crumple pieces of colorful construction paper into balls to represent scoops of ice cream. Store the "scoops" inside the ice cream cartons. Place the supplies in the center.

Directions: Encourage students to use their imaginations when ordering ice cream and remind workers to build the pretend sundaes with a smile. Everyone should always use good manners by saying, "Please," "Thank you," and "You're welcome."

🎭 Scene Selections

Supplies: index cards with prompts, card box, costumes, props, accessories

Setup: Write a prompt for a dramatic play experience on each index card. For example, *Take a ride on a magic flying carpet, Pretend you are on an African safari,* or *Imagine you are the first astronauts to travel to Mars.* Store the cards in the card box. Place the card box and other supplies in the center.

Directions: Have a student close his eyes and randomly select a card from the box. Depending on students' reading abilities, you may need to help them read the cards. Then, encourage students to build their dramatic play experience around that suggestion.

🌱 Fine Motor Skills Center ....

Activities completed in this center give students opportunities to develop fine motor skills. These activities include beading, manipulating small objects, molding dough, etc. Students will develop hand strength and muscle coordination, as well as hand-eye coordination and visual acuity skills. Many fine motor skills activities also prepare students developmentally for learning to write.

Some Suggested Supplies:

❀ small manipulatives (buttons, milk caps, coins, small toys, wooden beads, dry beans, uncooked pasta, etc.)
❀ soft manipulatives (cotton balls, craft pom-poms, small pieces of sponge, foam shapes, etc.)

❀ puzzles	❀ scissors	❀ writing utensils
❀ beads and yarn	❀ lacing boards	❀ collage materials
❀ molding dough	❀ tweezers	❀ eyedroppers
❀ cotton swabs	❀ magnets	❀ toys with knobs, switches, latches, or fasteners

Caution: Some small objects may present choking hazards and are not appropriate for children under age three.

Center Setup Tips:

❀ Label each bin with the name and a picture of each object that goes in it. Label the shelves, too, so that students will know where to put the bins when they clean up.
❀ If you are offering free time in the center, limit the number of containers that can be included in play to eliminate a lengthy cleanup.
❀ Plan a variety of activities so that students can practice many different skills and avoid becoming too familiar with each task.

Sample Center Activities

🌱 Sand Swirls

Supplies: liquid glue, small bowls of sand mixed with powdered tempera paint, construction paper
Setup: Fill a bowl with sand. Add two or three spoonfuls of powdered tempera paint and mix well. Prepare two more bowls of sand using different colors. Open the glue bottles slightly so that only a thin bead of glue will be released when squeezed.
Directions: Tell students to use the glue to quickly draw designs on their papers. When they have finished their designs, have each student pinch a small amount of sand and sprinkle it over her glue design. Let her continue pinching and sprinkling sand until all of the glue has been covered with sand. Help her gently tap the paper over the bowl to return any excess sand to the container. If the student wants to add another color of sand, have her add more glue and repeat the pinching and sprinkling process.

🌱 Tongs & Stuff

Supplies: several containers of small manipulatives, such as crayons, wooden beads, buttons, small figurines, etc.; empty bowls to collect the items; tongs or tweezers
Setup: Place the containers of manipulatives on a table next to the empty bowls. Or, for a challenge, place the empty bowls on the opposite side of the table.
Directions: Instruct students to use the tongs to move items from the containers to the empty bowls. Encourage each student to use only one hand while using the tongs and not to touch the manipulatives with his fingers. After a few minutes, have students use the tongs to remove the sorted objects from the bowls by counting each one as it is removed and placing it on the table. After all of the items have been counted, tell students to place the items back in their original containers using the tongs.

Variation: If students are struggling with this task, provide soft manipulatives that will be easier to grasp with tongs, such as cotton balls, craft pom-poms, or small pieces of sponge.

Gross Motor Skills Center..

The gross motor skills center allows students to explore using their large muscle groups—those in the arms, legs, torso, and back. Playing with equipment, such as balls, hoops, wagons, etc., provides opportunities to improve balance, hand-eye coordination, strength, and coordination. Additionally, it gives students a chance to run, jump, and play while using some of their boundless energy in an appropriate way.

Some Suggested Supplies:

❀ balls
❀ traffic cones
❀ large empty boxes
❀ laundry baskets
❀ jump ropes
❀ wagons, tricycles, and other ride-on toys
❀ large empty boxes
❀ plastic hoops

Center Setup Tips:

❀ Provide a large space for play and limit the number of students using the center at one time.
❀ Choose a variety of toys so that students can focus on two or three different gross motor skills at once.
❀ Provide a clearly labeled place to store the equipment when the activity is complete.

Sample Center Activities

Over, Under, & Around Obstacle Course

Supplies: assortment of obstacles, such as tables, chairs, boxes, laundry baskets, traffic cones, etc.

Setup: Place the obstacles throughout the play area. Or, have students place the obstacles to prepare the course.

Directions: Tell students to climb over, under, and around the obstacles. Students can play "follow the leader" through the obstacle course as the first student chooses the path, and the other classmates in the center follow him. Encourage students to take turns being the leader.

Extension: Extend the activity by introducing balls, beanbags, or balloons for partners to toss while navigating the course. (*Caution:* Before completing any balloon activity, ask families about possible latex allergies. Also, remember that uninflated or popped balloons may present a choking hazard.)

Curious Combos

Supplies: assortment of gross motor skills toys, such as balls, baskets, plastic hoops, ride-on toys, jump ropes, and traffic cones

Setup: Place the gross motor skills toys in the center area.

Directions: Encourage students to use the toys in the center in as many ways as possible. Give them very little instruction and let them create their own games and interactions using all of the toys.

🏠 Home Living Center...

The purpose of the home living center is to give students opportunities to explore tools and jobs that are common in home living and taking care of families. This center is especially effective when you provide child-sized furnishings and toy appliances so that everything is easily accessible and at eye level for students.

Some Suggested Supplies:

❀ toy kitchen appliances
❀ plastic dishes and utensils
❀ child-sized shelves and cabinets
❀ toy iron and ironing board
❀ toy cleaning supplies, such as dusting tools, a vacuum, a broom, and a dustpan

❀ child-sized table and chairs
❀ toy pots, pans, and cooking utensils
❀ dolls, doll bed, and clothes
❀ laundry basket

❀ table linens
❀ toy food
❀ dress-up clothes

Center Setup Tips:

❀ Students like to pretend to be adults; provide a large space so that several students can use the center at the same time.
❀ Encourage students to play a variety of roles so that everyone has opportunities to participate, regardless of gender.
❀ To avoid arguments over popular roles, create a system for randomly choosing who will play each role.

Sample Center Activities

🏠 Scene Suggestions

Supplies: index cards with prompts, card box, variety of home living supplies and accessories
Setup: Write a prompt for a home living scenario on each index card. For example, *Today is a student's first day of school, You are getting ready to go on vacation,* or *The family is preparing for someone's birthday party.* Store the cards in the card box. Place the card box and other supplies in the home living center.
Directions: Have a student close her eyes and randomly select a card from the box. Depending on students' reading abilities, you may need to help them read the cards. Then, encourage students to build their home living experience around that suggestion.

🏠 Neighborhood Life

Supplies: variety of home living supplies and accessories
Setup: Build a neighborhood around the room by creating other dramatic play centers to complement the home living center. For example, you might include a grocery store, a post office, a gas station, and a school. Select the types of neighborhood locations that you want to build. Set up the centers around the room as space allows. Consider using cardboard appliance boxes to create additional buildings, tables, and appliances. Students can help you decorate the boxes accordingly using crayons, markers, and paint.
Directions: Help students choose which centers they will play in and select their roles. If you have space and the supplies to create more centers, a large number of students can be involved at one time. Make sure you monitor students' movement as they visit the centers. You do not want one neighborhood location to become overcrowded and another to be left empty.

🍳 Kitchen Center...

The kitchen center allows students to explore and have fun with food. In addition to learning independence, they will experience new tastes, develop small motor skills, use numbers and number concepts, and experiment with different textures. Encourage students to try everything they make.

Caution: Before completing any food activity, ask families' permission and inquire about students' food allergies and religious or other food preferences.

Some Suggested Supplies:

- plastic utensils
- mixing bowls and spoons
- child-sized chef hats
- paper or plastic plates and bowls
- measuring cups and spoons
- cleaning supplies, such as wipes, paper towels, soap, sponges, etc.
- resealable plastic bags
- aprons or smocks

Center Setup Tips:

- Keep the activities simple. Recipes should include two or three steps for preschool students and no more than five steps for kindergarten students.
- Create a cookbook using blank recipe cards or index cards so that students have a reference to use in the center. Include simple icons or drawings for students who are still learning to read.
- Demonstrate and reinforce the need for safety and sanitation. Students must always wash their hands before working in the kitchen center and clean the work surfaces before and after working in the kitchen center. Also, remind students not to waste food; they should eat what they prepare.

Sample Center Activities

🍳 Fruit Dip

Supplies: bowls, spoons, fruit, vanilla yogurt, whipped topping
Setup: Have students wash the fruit while you cut it into bite-sized pieces. Or, wash and cut the fruit in advance. Place the yogurt, whipped topping, and fruit pieces in bowls on the table. Provide a spoon for each bowl. Give each student a bowl and a spoon.
Directions: Provide an illustrated recipe card with the following steps on it. Explain the steps to students as you demonstrate the activity. Each student should then follow the recipe.
1. Measure 2 large spoonfuls of yogurt into your bowl.
2. Measure 1 large spoonful of whipped topping into your bowl.
3. Stir the mixture well.
4. Dip your fruit pieces into your fruit dip and enjoy your snack!

🍳 PB & J Pizza

Supplies: rolling pin, plates, plastic spoons or knives, bread, peanut butter, jelly, dried fruits, nuts
Setup: Place the ingredients and supplies on the table. Provide plastic spoons or knives to spread the peanut butter and jelly. Include spoons for the dried fruits and nuts.
Directions: Provide an illustrated recipe card with the following steps on it. Explain the steps to students as you demonstrate the activity. Each student should then follow the recipe.
1. Gently roll the rolling pin over your slice of bread to flatten it a little.
2. Spread some peanut butter on your bread.
3. Spread some jelly on top of the peanut butter.
4. Sprinkle some dried fruit or nuts on top of the jelly.
5. Enjoy your snack!

◇ Library Center...

The library center provides an opportunity for students to experience literature. Students are able to interact with letters and words while learning about how books are written, illustrated, and printed. The primary purpose of the center is for students to spend time with books. Therefore, you will find literature suggestions in each chapter of themed activities (pages 21–78) instead of actual activities to complete in the library center.

Some Suggested Supplies:
❀ age-appropriate fiction and nonfiction books of all shapes and sizes
❀ seats, such as chairs, pillows, beanbag chairs, etc.
❀ bookshelf   ❀ checkout system   ❀ stuffed animals to read to or with

Center Setup Tips:
❀ Include a variety of books, such as picture books, comic books, board books, interactive books, pop-up books, and books featuring photography, to engage students' many different interests.
❀ Provide plenty of comfortable places for reading. Beanbag chairs, small upholstered chairs, large floor pillows, and soft rugs are all warm and inviting spots in which to curl up with a book.
❀ Teach students how to handle and care for books.
❀ Create a checkout system that students can use even if they are still learning to read. Cut blank sentence strips into bookmark-sized lengths. Make a small copy of each book's cover. Glue a copy of a book cover to the end of each bookmark and write the title of the book below the picture. Place each bookmark inside the front cover of the corresponding book. Create a separate poster with a labeled library pocket for each student. To check out a book, a student should remove the bookmark from the front of the book and place it in his pocket on the poster. When returning a book, the student should put the bookmark back in the book.

Sample Center Activities

◇ Library Scavenger Hunt
Supplies: enlarged photocopies of pictures or illustrations from several books in the library center
Setup: Choose three to five pictures or illustrations and hang them on the wall above the bookshelf in the library center.
Directions: Tell students to look for pictures or illustrations while they are reading in the library center. When students find the pictures or illustrations that are on display, have them let you know. Consider rewarding them with stickers or small prizes if they can tell you what is happening in the illustrations based on what they have read so far. (Students need to provide this explanation; otherwise, they might simply flip through the books to find the pictures or illustrations without reading the text.)

Extension: Place a word and a picture icon on the wall, such as a picture of a dog with the word *dog* written below it. Have students search the books they are reading to find stories about the highlighted picture and word.

◇ 👂 Mystery Reader Read-Along
Supplies: tape recorder with headphones, tapes, books
Setup: Combine the library center with the listening center (page 13) by creating a mystery reader read-along. Choose a variety of people who are familiar to students, such as parents who visit the classroom often, the school director or principal, cafeteria personnel, gym teachers, etc. Ask these people to record themselves reading stories from the center. Have them ring a bell or sound a beep at the end of each page to help students read along as they are listening to the stories.
Directions: Have each student choose a book. Help her start the tape that corresponds with the book. The student should read along in the book as she listens to the tape through the headphones. At the end of the story, have her guess who the mystery reader is.

Listening Center..

The listening center provides an opportunity for students to learn through listening. Activities completed in the listening center help students learn to focus, use their imaginations, and explore the world through their auditory senses.

Some Suggested Supplies:
* variety of music genres
* headphones
* books on tape or CD
* tape or CD players

Center Setup Tips:
* Place the listening center in a quiet corner so that students have an atmosphere that is conducive to listening.
* Headphones, tape and CD players, and all tapes and CDs should be labeled and color coded so that students can operate them safely and easily. For example, on a tape player put a red dot sticker on the stop button, a green dot sticker on the play button, etc.
* Mark the volume control (or limit it if possible) so that students cannot accidentally turn the volume to a level that could damage their hearing.

Sample Center Activities

Listen & Match
Supplies: assortment of objects that make sounds, such as bells, whistles, kazoos, a toy piano, a telephone, etc.; premade tape; tape player; headphones
Setup: Prepare a tape by recording the sound of each object, one at a time. Leave long pauses between the sounds. Place the supplies on a table in the center.
Directions: Tell students to spread the noise-making objects on the table. As they listen to the sounds on the tape, they should try to match the sounds to the objects on the table. Have students arrange the objects in the order that they are played and then compare their results with a classmate.

Illustrating to Music
Supplies: paper, crayons, premade tape, tape player, headphones
Setup: Prepare a tape with several short clips of a variety of music genres, such as a snappy classical march, a quiet lullaby, a western ballad, etc. Leave long pauses between the clips. Place the supplies on a table in the center.
Directions: Encourage students to draw, color, or scribble in time with the mood and beat as they listen to the music. Tell them to choose the colors of their crayons based on the moods of the music. Have them use new pieces of paper for each genre of music.

123 Math & Numbers Center ....

The math and numbers center provides opportunities for students to explore numbers, size and quantity comparisons, number recognition, and quantifying sets of objects. Through activities involving manipulating objects and numbers, students will gain skills and confidence in counting, learning ordinal numbers, reasoning, estimation, and fine motor skills.

Some Suggested Supplies:

- ❀ calculators
- ❀ number cards
- ❀ scale
- ❀ counters
- ❀ flash cards
- ❀ paper
- ❀ rulers
- ❀ fair number cubes
- ❀ pencils
- ❀ playing cards
- ❀ balance
- ❀ coins or money manipulatives

Center Setup Tips:

- ❀ When students are sorting, counting, and manipulating objects in the math and numbers center, encourage them to write and record the numbers as they work. For example, if students are counting beans, have them record the total number of beans that they count.
- ❀ Provide a container with deep sides for each center participant when students will be rolling fair number cubes or sorting counters. This will keep the activity contained and make cleanup easier.

Sample Center Activities

123 Patterning

Supplies: index cards; variety of common items with recognizable shapes, such as a game board (square), a clock (circle), a toy slice of pizza (triangle), etc.

Setup: Make three index cards for each shape that students are able to recognize. Draw the shapes on the cards. Shuffle the cards. Place the cards and the items on a table in the center.

Directions: Each student should draw two or three cards from the stack and place them on the table in front of her. These cards represent a pattern. The student should then choose items from the box to create a pattern that matches the one shown on the cards. Have the student repeat the activity with new cards and new objects after each pattern has been completed.

123 Shake & Match

Supplies: empty, clean, plastic foam egg cartons (without holes in them); marbles; dried beans

Setup: Using a permanent marker, write a number from 1 to 12 in the bottom of each cup of the egg cartons. The numbers should be written in random order. Place the cartons and other supplies on a table in the center.

Directions: Each student visiting the center will need two egg cartons. Have a student place one marble inside an egg carton and close the lid. Tell him to shake it gently and then open the top. The student should read the number on the bottom of the cup where the marble has landed. Then, he should find the matching number in his second egg carton and place that number of dried beans in the cup. Have students continue shaking and matching until all of the numbers have been correctly identified and matched or until a set length of time has lapsed.

♪ Music Center...

The music center provides an opportunity for students to explore music through various musical instruments and presentations. In addition to auditory discrimination, students develop fine motor skills and listening skills in the music center. Students can also begin to determine which types of music they prefer and why.

Some Suggested Supplies:
❀ variety of musical instruments (purchased or homemade)
❀ items that can be used as instruments, such as pots, pans, spoons, empty coffee cans, etc.
❀ variety of bells ❀ tape or CD player ❀ tapes or CDs

Center Setup Tips:
❀ Provide an assortment of musical instruments, as well as nontraditional noisemakers so that students have a variety of choices.
❀ You may also wish to provide several of each type of instrument so that more than one student can play at one time.
❀ Alternate choices frequently so that only a few types of instruments are offered each day. Then, students will be encouraged to try a variety of instruments instead of always selecting the same favorites.

Sample Center Activities

♪ Rhythm Shakers
Supplies: tape or CD player; tapes or CDs; empty, clean, plastic water bottles with lids; paper; dried beans; uncooked rice; small jingle bells; chenille stems; stickers
Setup: Using the directions below, make a rhythm shaker to display as a reference for students. Place the supplies on a table in the center.
Directions: Help each student fashion a funnel with a piece of paper and use it to pour dried beans and uncooked rice into her water bottle. Place the lid tightly on the bottle. Have each student string two or three jingle bells onto a chenille stem and twist it tightly around the neck of the bottle. Let students decorate their bottles with stickers. To play, encourage students to shake or tap their bottles on their hands, hips, and the table to hear the rattling and jingling. Play music and encourage students to shake the bottles to the beat.

♪ Songwriters
Supplies: instruments that are color coded by note, such as colorful handbells, xylophones with colorful bars, etc.; enlarged copy of the Musical Staff Pattern (page 16); colorful construction paper circles
Setup: You will need one piece of construction paper in each color that is represented on the instruments. Cut several 1" (2.5 cm) circles from each piece of paper. Laminate the circles and Musical Staff Pattern for durability. Attach hook-and-loop tape to the backs of the circles and to the front of the Musical Staff Pattern. Hang the Musical Staff Pattern on a wall in the center. Place the circles and the instruments on a table.
Directions: Explain to students that the colorful circles represent musical notes and each color corresponds to a note. Play a few notes to demonstrate their different sounds. Have students attach the circles to the lines and spaces on the musical staff in any order they wish. Then, tell students to play the song by following the notes in the sequence, matching the colors of the notes to the colors on the instruments.

Variation: Assign each student one color. Let students practice their cooperation skills by playing the song together, each playing only the note for his assigned color.

Musical Staff Pattern

Activities found on pages 15, 67, and 77.

 Science Center

The science center provides opportunities for students to explore, observe, test, and discover at their own pace. In addition to developing fine motor skills and cognitive thinking skills, working in the science center teaches students about observational concepts, such as cause and effect, and comparing and contrasting.

Caution: Before completing any nature activity, ask families' permission and inquire about students' plant and animal allergies. Remind students not to touch potentially harmful plants or animals during the activity.

Some Suggested Supplies:

- magnifying glass
- paper plates, cups, bowls
- plastic funnels
- tweezers
- protective eyewear
- empty storage containers with lids
- plastic utensils
- balance
- eyedroppers
- cleaning supplies, such as wipes, paper towels, soap, sponges, etc.
- resealable plastic bags
- plastic beakers and test tubes
- scale
- lab coats, aprons, or smocks

Center Setup Tips:

- Discuss the safety rules of the science center, such as keeping all of the tools and substances in their proper containers, wearing aprons or smocks and protective eyewear, no tasting of substances, etc.
- Scientists always document their work. Provide a science lab book for each student so that she can write, dictate, and draw about the things she explores in the science center. Create the lab books by making one copy of the Lab Book Pattern (page 18). Cut out the large rectangle along the dotted line. Enlarge and make 10 copies for each student. Fold the copies in half and staple along the folded edge. Write *(student's name)'s Science Center Lab Book* on the outside front cover of each book.
- Store the lab books in a box in the science center so that students can use them each time they visit.

Sample Center Activities

 Moving Droplets

Supplies: lab books, pencils and crayons, bowls of colorful water, eyedroppers, plastic drinking straws, waxed paper

Setup: Fill the bowl half full of water. Add three to five drops of food coloring to tint the water. Tear off a piece of waxed paper that is approximately the size of a place mat for each student who will be visiting the center. Place the supplies on a table in the center.

Directions: Have each student use an eyedropper to place a few drops of colorful water on his waxed paper. Then, he should use a straw to gently blow air to move the droplets around on the paper. Encourage students to think about how the air from the straw is pushing the water and causing it to move. Have students try to move the droplets in a certain direction. Then, have students write or draw their observations in their lab books.

 Nature Box

Supplies: lab books; pencils and crayons; box of items from nature, such as pinecones, feathers, acorns, dirt, insects in jars with holes in the lids, leaves, etc.; tweezers; magnifying glass

Setup: Place the items from nature in the box. If you use insect jars, set them upright and provide plenty of food and environmental comforts for the insects. Remember to set the insects free outside as soon as center time is complete. Place the supplies on a table in the center.

Directions: Encourage students to use tweezers to carefully pick up each item if needed. Many items can be picked up without tweezers. Have students use a magnifying glass to observe each of the items. Remind them not to remove the lids from the insect jars. They can observe the insects through the sides of the jars using the magnifying glass. Ask students to consider the similarities and differences among the items they observe. Then, have them draw pictures of two or three items in their lab books. If they wish, they can draw the items as they appear when observed through a magnifying glass.

Lab Book Pattern

Assembly instructions found on page 17.

I learned . . .

(fold here)

I learned . . .

Sensory Center...

The sensory center provides opportunities for students to explore different media through sight, sound, smell, and touch. As they work in the center, students will also have opportunities to manipulate objects while developing abstract and concrete thought processes. Students will become aware of how the senses are interconnected when they complete activities that engage more than one sense at a time.

Caution: Some sensory center activities include leaves, pinecones, feathers, and other items from nature. Before completing any nature activity, ask families' permission and inquire about students' plant and animal allergies. Remind students not to touch potentially harmful plants or animals during the activity.

Some Suggested Supplies:
- sensory table (also known as a sand or water table) or large plastic container
- tarp or mat to protect the floor
- aprons or smocks
- measuring cups
- spoons
- bowls and other containers
- strainers
- items to look at, listen to, smell, touch, sift, and pour, such as cotton balls, uncooked pasta, powdered drink mixes, cooking extracts, small manipulatives, dried beans, flour, water, packing peanuts, etc.

Center Setup Tips:
- Make sure the sensory table is large enough for more than one student to play and interact at the same time.
- Place the sensory table at a comfortable height for students to use when standing so that they will have easy access to its contents.
- Place a large mat or tarp underneath the sensory table to contain spills.
- Remind students never to put an item from the sensory table into their mouths and to always wash their hands before and after playing in the center.
- Recycle sensory center materials for art or science projects whenever possible.

Sample Center Activities

Touch & Guess Boxes
Supplies: several shoe boxes with lids; variety of familiar objects with unique and distinguishable shapes and textures, such as an orange, a hair brush, a stuffed animal, a pinecone, a rock, a sock, etc.

Setup: Wrap the boxes and tops separately with craft or wrapping paper. (The lids should be removable without having to tear the paper.) Cut a hole large enough for a child's hand in the side of each box. Place one item inside each box and cover it with the lid. If desired, temporarily secure the lids in place with rubber bands. Place the boxes on a table in the center.

Directions: Have each student poke his hand through the hole in a box and feel the object inside. Tell him to decide what item is in the box. Encourage students to use descriptive words to talk about the objects that they feel. After they have finished guessing, remove the rubber bands and let them check their answers.

Texture Families
Supplies: 4 large bins or baskets; variety of textured items that are bumpy, smooth, rough, or soft
Setup: Place the supplies on a table in the center.
Directions: Tell students to sort the items into the bins according to their textures. For example, all of the smooth objects would go in one bin, all of the bumpy objects in another bin, etc.

✏ Writing Center.....................................

The writing center provides opportunities for students to explore different writing techniques and tools while experimenting with letters, letter shapes, words, and sentences. Activities completed in the writing center foster fine motor skills and pre-reading skills, as well as offer opportunities for self-expression and creativity.

Some Suggested Supplies:

- ❀ variety of paper
- ❀ computer
- ❀ word and letter stencils
- ❀ variety of writing tools
- ❀ word and letter stamps
- ❀ word and letter stickers
- ❀ typewriter
- ❀ ink pads

Center Setup Tips:

- ❀ Provide an assortment of papers, including a variety of colors, shapes, textures, and sizes.
- ❀ Occasionally, provide dimensional objects to write on instead of paper, such as boxes, cups, bowls, or other containers.
- ❀ Provide an assortment of writing tools, such as pencils, pens, markers, crayons, pastels, and chalk.
- ❀ Occasionally, provide unconventional writing tools, such as lipsticks, cotton swabs and paints, glitter glue, or shaving foam.

Sample Center Activities

✏ Word Cards

Supplies: word cards, sentence strips with writing lines, pencils or crayons, large construction paper, tape

Setup: Create word cards by writing the names of familiar objects, such as *book*, *dog*, *doll*, *cat*, *table*, *door*, etc., on index cards. Cut the sentence strips into fourths. Place the supplies on a table in the center.

Directions: Have each student select a word card and carefully copy the word onto a piece of sentence strip. Then, have her use the word in a sentence. For example, if she makes a *dog* word strip, ask her to tell you what she knows about dogs. Write her sentence on a large piece of construction paper and let her tape her word strip to the paper in the correct place in the sentence.

✏ Squiggle Trails

Supplies: copies of prepared line designs, assortment of colorful writing tools

Setup: Create several pages of simple line designs by drawing squiggles, zigzags, and straight lines on pieces of paper. Keep the designs simple and avoid intersecting the lines. Make several copies of each squiggle trail sample. Place the copies and writing tools on a table in the center.

Directions: Encourage students to use an assortment of writing tools to trace the lines on each of the different squiggle trail pages. Have them use different tools for each type of trail. For example, a student might use a blue crayon for straight lines, a red glitter pen for curvy lines, and an orange marker for zigzags.

All About Me

🎨 Favorite Color Collages . . . .

Supplies: colorful collage supplies, such as chenille stems, craft pom-poms, foam shapes, craft feathers, buttons, yarn, craft paper, crayons and markers, colorful uncooked pasta, magazines, etc.; glue; scissors; construction paper

Setup: Place the supplies on a table in the center.

Directions: Have each student select a piece of construction paper in her favorite color. Then, help her write *My favorite color is . . .* at the top of the paper. Let each student use the collage supplies that are this same favorite color to create her own masterpiece. Encourage students to search the magazines for pictures of objects that are the same color and glue them to the collages, as well.

🏠 It Looks Just Like Me! . . . .

Supplies: blocks in a variety of shapes and sizes

Setup: Place the blocks in the center.

Directions: Encourage students to use the blocks to create self-portrait structures. They will probably find it easier to create the structures as silhouettes lying on the floor rather than three-dimensional figures. Remind them to try to make the figures life-sized!

◇ Library Literature . . . .

I Like Me! by Nancy Carlson (Puffin Books, 1990)
I Like Myself! by Karen Beaumont (Scholastic, Inc., 2005)
I'm Gonna Like Me: Letting Off a Little Self-Esteem by Jamie Lee Curtis (Joanna Cotler, 2002)
My Book about Me (Classic Seuss) by Dr. Seuss and Roy McKie (Random House Books for Young Readers, 1969)
The Way I Feel by Janan Cain (Scholastic, 2000)

🎧 🎨 Listen & Draw . . . .

Supplies: paper, crayons, mirror, premade tape, tape player, headphones

Setup: Prepare a tape of your voice giving instructions for drawing a self-portrait. For example, you might say, "Look in the mirror. How is your head shaped? Stop the tape while you draw the shape on your paper. [*Pause.*] What color is your hair? How does it look? Stop the tape while you draw your hair on your paper. [*Pause.*]," etc. Place the supplies on a table in the center.

Directions: Instruct students to listen to the tape and follow the directions to draw self-portraits. Tell them that they will be asked to stop the tape frequently while they are drawing.

21

123 "How Many?" Mini-Book . . . .

Supplies: copies of the "How Many?" Mini-Book (page 23), crayons, digital scale, large blocks

Setup: Make a copy of the "How Many?" Mini-Book for each student. Cut along the dotted lines and staple the pages together to make a mini-book for each student. Place the supplies in the center.

Directions: Give each student a mini-book. Help her write her name on the mini-book. Have each student complete the following steps to fill in her mini-book.

1. Color the title page and write as many numbers as you can in the empty space.
2. Count the number of fingers on your hand and write that number on page 1.
3. Stand on a scale. Write how much you weigh on the scale and in the blank on page 2.
4. Stack blocks in a tower that is as tall as you are. Count how many blocks are in the tower. Write the number of blocks on page 3.

♪ One Person Band . . . .

Supplies: variety of musical instruments, such as a drum, a kazoo, wood blocks, etc.

Setup: Place the instruments on a table in the center.

Directions: Encourage each student who visits the center to compose a song that requires use of all of the instruments on the table. Challenge students to find a way to play more than one instrument at a time.

🍃 Fingerprint Exploration . . . .

Supplies: lab books, pencils and crayons, ink pads with washable ink, index cards, magnifying glasses

Setup: Find 8 to 10 volunteers. Have each volunteer make a fingerprint on two index cards. All of the volunteers should use the same finger when making the prints. Code the cards on the backs so that students will be able to match them. For example, on the back of each of one volunteer's cards, place a red dot, on the back of each of another volunteer's cards, place a blue dot, etc. Laminate the cards for durability. Place the cards and supplies on a table in the center.

Directions: Talk to students about how fingerprints are made and the fact that everyone's fingerprints are unique. Let students use the ink pads to make several fingerprints in their lab books. Then, after they have washed their hands, let students examine the fingerprint cards with the magnifying glasses. Have students try to find the matching cards by comparing the prints. Have them check their answers by comparing the color coded dots on the backs of the cards.

✏️ 🎨 My Name Is Special . . . .

Supplies: letter stamps, ink pads with washable ink, paper

Setup: Write each student's name at the top of a piece of paper. If desired, use the Internet to research the meaning of each student's name and write it at the bottom of the piece of paper. Place the supplies on a table in the center.

Directions: When students come to the center, have them find their pieces of paper. Then, talk to them about their names and how special their names are. If you included the meanings of the names, discuss that information, as well. Let each student use the letter stamps to spell his name on the piece of paper while using the written name as a guide. Students can also spell the names of friends, family members, or pets using the stamps.

"How Many?" Mini-Book

Activity found on page 22.

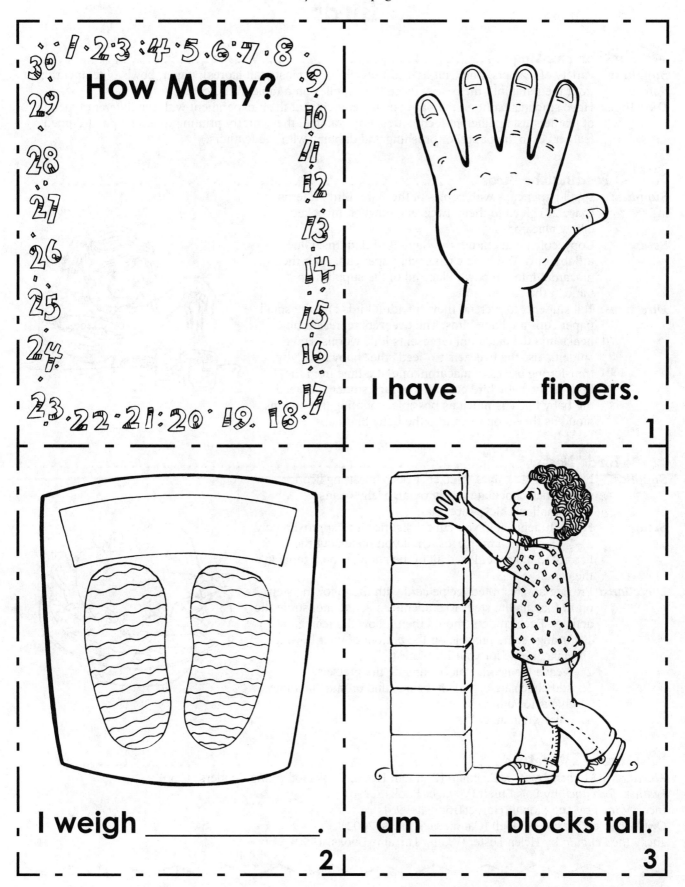

30 1 2 3 4 5 6 7 8 9
29 10
28 11
27 12
26 13
25 14
24 15
23 22 21 20 19 18 17 16

How Many?

I have _____ fingers.

1

I weigh _____.

2

I am _____ blocks tall.

3

CD-104198 *It's Center Time!*

Birds

🎨 Feather Painting . . . .

Supplies: variety of feathers, both soft and stiff (available at most craft stores); paper; bowls of tempera paint
Setup: Pour the paint into the bowls. Place the supplies on a table in the center.
Directions: Have students paint on the paper using feathers. Let them experiment with the different types of feathers using different techniques. For example, they can try printing (pressing paint-dipped feathers onto the paper) or brushing and dabbing with the feathers.

🐛 123 Feeding the Birds . . . .

Supplies: small paper cups with copies of the Baby Bird Patterns (page 26) glued to them, tweezers, bowl of uncooked elbow macaroni

Setup: Copy, color, and cut out the Baby Bird Patterns. Glue a Baby Bird Pattern to each small paper cup. Pour the macaroni into the bowl. Place all of the supplies on a table in the center.

Directions: Tell students to pretend they are adult birds and the small paper cups are baby birds. The tweezers represent bird beaks and the macaroni represents little worms. Have students use the tweezers to "feed" the "baby birds" by transferring pieces of macaroni one at a time from the bowl to the baby bird cups. Encourage students to feed the baby birds as much as possible, counting the "worms" aloud as they drop them into the baby bird cups.

👨‍🍳 🐛 Birds' Nests . . . .

Supplies: bowls, plastic knives, pretzel sticks, shoestring licorice, egg-shaped chocolate candy or large jelly beans, marshmallow chicks (optional)

Setup: Have students help you cut the licorice into approximately 2"–3" (5 cm–7.5 cm) pieces. Or, if you prefer, cut the licorice in advance. Place all of the supplies on a table in the center.

Directions: Provide an illustrated recipe card with the following steps on it. Explain the steps to students as you demonstrate the activity. Each student should then follow the recipe.
1. Arrange some pretzels on the bottom of your bowl to make a base for your bird's nest.
2. Weave the licorice pieces among the pretzels.
3. Add chocolate eggs, jelly beans, and/or marshmallow chicks to your nest.
4. Enjoy your snack!

🔷 Library Literature . . . .

Are You My Mother? by P. D. Eastman (Random House Books for Young Readers, 1960)
Feathers for Lunch by Lois Ehlert (Voyager Books, 1996)
Inch by Inch by Leo Lionni (HarperTrophy, 1995)
Owl Babies by Martin Waddell (Candlewick Press, 2002)
Tacky the Penguin by Helen Lester (Walter Lorraine Books, 1990)

123 Count & Fill Eggs

Supplies: large basket of plastic eggs, index cards cut into fourths, cups, jelly beans, bowl

Setup: Write a number from 1 to 5 on each piece of index card. Put one numbered piece of index card inside each plastic egg. Put all of the eggs in the basket and the jelly beans in the bowl. Place all of the supplies on a table in the center.

Directions: Have each student select five eggs from the basket. Tell her to open the eggs one at a time and read the numbers on the cards. For each number, she should place that many jelly beans in her cup. After she has opened the five eggs and put the jelly beans into the cup, have her remove all of the jelly beans from the cup and count them to find the total.

Bird Watching

Supplies: lab books, pencils and crayons, photographs of birds from magazines, child-sized binoculars

Setup: Display the bird photographs on the walls of the center. Place the supplies on a table in the center.

Directions: Tell students to observe the bird photographs with and without the binoculars. Encourage them to study each bird and try to name three things that are interesting or different about each bird. Have students draw pictures of their favorite birds in their lab books and write or dictate about the interesting characteristics they noticed.

Extension: Place a bird feeder outside a classroom window. Let students use the binoculars to study the birds that visit the feeder. Have students draw pictures and write or dictate stories about the birds they observe. (See Observing Bird Feeders activity, page 56.)

Feathers

Supplies: sensory table; variety of feathers in different sizes, textures, and colors (available at most craft stores)

Setup: Place the feathers in the sensory table in the center.

Directions: Encourage students to sink their hands into the feathers. Tell them to look carefully at the different kinds of feathers and talk to each other about the similarities and differences they notice.

Robins & Nests

Supplies: copies of the Robin and Nest Patterns (page 26), crayons, scissors, glue, construction paper

Setup: Make enlarged copies of the Robin and Nest Patterns (page 26) for each student. Count the number of letters in each student's name. You will need one copy for every three letters. For example, Alexander would need three copies of the Robin and Nest Patterns because he has nine letters in his name. Make sure you enlarge the patterns so that students can easily write one letter on each robin or egg. Place the supplies on a table in the center.

Directions: Have each student write his name in uppercase letters, one letter on each robin. Then, have him write his name in lowercase letters, one letter on each egg. Let students color the robins and nests as desired and cut out the squares along the dotted lines. Tell students to glue their nests in order on a piece of construction paper. Then, they should match the robins to the nests and glue them in place, as well.

Baby Bird, Robin, & Nest Patterns

Activities found on pages 24–25.

Dinosaurs

🎨 What Did They Look Like? . . . .

Supplies: copies of the Dinosaur Pattern (page 29); crayons; markers; collage materials, such as sequins, glitter, yarn scraps, dried beans, buttons, feathers, uncooked pasta, etc.; glue

Setup: Make a copy of the Dinosaur Pattern page for each student on heavy paper. Place the supplies on a table in the center.

Directions: Explain to students that since dinosaurs are extinct, no one really knows what color they were or what they looked like. Encourage students to color their dinosaurs and add details, such as trees, grass, other dinosaurs, the sky, etc. Then, let them use the collage materials to embellish the dinosaurs. When students have completed their projects, have them name their dinosaurs and help them write the names at the tops of the pages.

🎭 🎨 Dinosaur Suits . . . .

Supplies: dinosaur suit and headband for each student; crayons; markers; construction paper; glue

Setup: Use brown and green bulletin board paper to create paper trees and blue bulletin board paper to make large blue shapes to represent ponds. Tape the trees and ponds to the walls and floor in the center. Prepare a dinosaur suit and a headband for each student (see illustration). Place the suits and headbands on a table in the center with the other supplies.

For a suit: Cut out one side of a large paper grocery bag. Cut the removed piece into a triangle to make a tail and staple it to the back side of the bag. Cut out a semi-circle from the bottom of the bag for a neck hole. Cut arm holes in the sides of the bag. A student will wear the suit like a vest with the open side in the front. For a headband: Cut the middle out of a paper plate, leaving a ring that is 2" (5 cm) wide. Cut out a section of the ring, approximately 4" (10 cm) long. Punch one hole in each end of the remaining portion of the ring and tie a 12" (30 cm) length of yarn through each hole. A student will wear the headband like a visor and tie it securely in the back with the two pieces of yarn.

Directions: Have students decorate their dinosaur suits. Encourage them to color, cut, and glue construction paper spikes and scales to the backs of their suits. Let them cut and glue triangle spikes around the edges of their headbands. Help students put on their dinosaur suits and tie the headbands onto their heads. Let students explore the dinosaur habitat in the dramatic play center.

◇ Library Literature . . . .

Count-a-saurus by Nancy Blumenthal (Aladdin, 1992)
Danny and the Dinosaur by Syd Hoff (HarperTrophy, 1992)
Dinosaur Roar! by Henrietta Stickland and Paul Stickland (Puffin, 2002)
How Do Dinosaurs Say Good Night? by Jane Yolen (HarperCollins, 2002)
My Big Dinosaur Book by Roger Priddy (Priddy Books, 2004)

Dinosaur Romp

Supplies: two-sided footprint sign, bell, dinosaur suits and headbands (optional; directions on page 27)

Setup: Trace or draw six dinosaur footprints, approximately 5" (13 cm) in diameter, on construction paper and cut them out. Glue two footprints on one side of a piece of sturdy card stock and draw a large number 2 at the top of the page. Glue four footprints on the back of the card stock and draw a large number 4 at the top of the page. Laminate the card stock for durability. Glue the card stock to a paint stirring stick to make a two-sided sign. Place the sign and the bell on a table in the center.

Directions: Have students put on their dinosaur suits and headbands (optional). Let one student be in charge of the sign and bell. Have the other students pretend to be dinosaurs. Tell the student with the sign to hold it up for her classmates to see. If she shows the side with two footprints, the "dinosaurs" should stomp around on two legs and growl. When she changes the sign to show four footprints, she should ring the bell to notify the dinosaurs of the change. They should then change to four-legged dinosaurs and romp around looking for food. Have students trade places after a few turns so that everyone gets a chance to be a dinosaur.

123 Dino Dominoes

Supplies: 24 dinosaur dominoes

Setup: Make 24 index card dominoes by drawing a line across the middle of each card with a black marker. Lay the cards in front of you. You have 48 sections (2 sections per card). Randomly select 8 sections and place 1 small dinosaur sticker in each section. Repeat this process using 2, 3, 4, 5, and 6 stickers. Laminate the cards for durability. Place the dino dominoes on a table in the center.

Directions: Tell students to shuffle the dominoes and place them facedown on the table. The first player should select a domino and turn it over. Player two selects a second domino. If it has a side with the same number of dinosaur stickers to match the first domino, players should align the dominoes so that the matching sections touch. Players continue drawing and matching until all of the domino cards have been used.

Fossil Dig

Supplies: sensory table prepared for a fossil dig, paintbrushes, plastic knives and spoons, 2 sand pails or bowls

Setup: Fill the sensory table with sand. Bury several small dinosaur figurines and manipulative toys in the sand. Place the other supplies on top of the sand.

Directions: Talk to students about archaeology and how scientists must dig very carefully when they are looking for dinosaur fossils. Explain that students will be archaeologists and look for fossils in the sand. Tell them to use the knives, spoons, and paintbrushes to carefully search for objects in the sand. They should sort all of the dinosaurs into one pail and all of the other objects into the second pail.

Dino Rub

Supplies: copies of the Dinosaur Pattern (page 29); crayons; assortment of items with textured surfaces, such as sandpaper, a door mat, linoleum, tile, a concrete stepping stone, etc.

Setup: Place the supplies on a table in the center.

Directions: Have each student place a Dinosaur Pattern over one of the textured surfaces. He should rub a crayon over the paper to create a textured "skin" for the dinosaur. Encourage students to try different textures for different parts of the dinosaur and to use the textures when creating a background around the dinosaur.

Dinosaur Pattern

Activities found on pages 27–28.

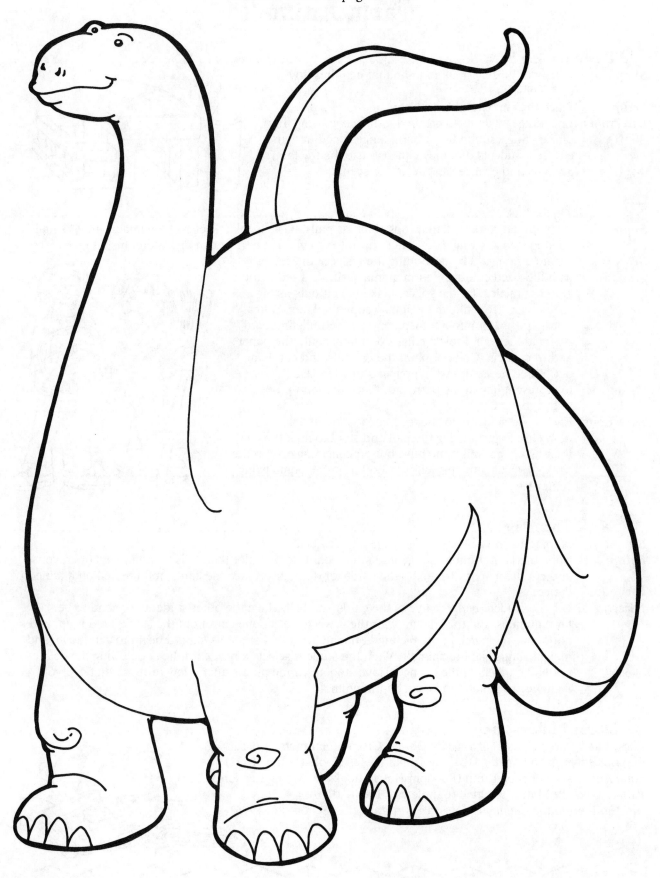

Farm Animals

🏠 Down on the Farm . . . .

Supplies: variety of blocks, small farm animal figurines, toy farm vehicles

Setup: Place the supplies in the center.

Directions: Encourage students to create a farm scene using the blocks. Suggest building a barn, fences, feed troughs, etc. Tell students that they can also use the toy farm animals and vehicles as part of the scene.

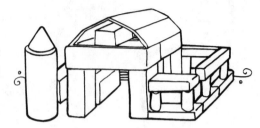

🎭 🏠 Farmyard . . . .

Supplies: farm animal cutouts; farm props, such as pails, baskets, plastic eggs, homemade "hay," small milking stools, a wagon, a butter churn (or a cylindrical trash can and a broomstick), etc.

Setup: Create a farmyard by decorating the walls of the center with life-sized cutouts of farm animals. (If life-sized cutouts are not practical for the space, make the cutouts as big as you can.) To make the animals, copy the Farm Animal Cards (page 32) onto a transparency. Tape bulletin board paper to the wall. Project enlarged animals onto the paper and trace them. Color or paint the animals and cut them out. Shred newsprint with a paper shredder. Use it to represent hay in the barnyard. Place the farm props in the center.

Directions: Encourage students to choose roles to play in the farmyard. Suggest using the pail and stool to milk the cow, then using the "milk" to churn butter; collecting eggs in the baskets; feeding the pig leftover food from the home living center; etc.

👟 Walk This Way . . . .

Supplies: prepared Farm Animal Cards (page 32), cowbell

Setup: Copy the Farm Animal Cards onto sturdy card stock. Color the cards with markers or crayons and cut them apart. Laminate the cards for durability. Place the cards and the bell on a table in the center.

Directions: Let one student be in charge of the cards and bell. Have the other students pretend to be farm animals. Tell the student with the cards to select one card from the stack, hold it up, and announce the name of the pictured animal. The other students should begin to act, move, and make sounds like the animal. When the student selects a new card, he should ring the bell to notify the others of the change. Have students trade places after a few turns so that everyone gets a chance to pretend to be each farm animal.

📖 Library Literature . . . .

Click, Clack, Moo: Cows That Type by Doreen Cronin (Gardners Books, 2003)
The Day Jimmy's Boa Ate the Wash by Trinka Hakes Noble (Puffin, 1992)
Farm Animals by Phoebe Dunn (Random House Books for Young Readers, 1984)
Farmer Duck by Martin Waddell (Candlewick Press, 1996)
Inside a Barn in the Country by Alyssa Satin Capucilli (Scholastic, 1995)

30

♫ Who Said That?

Supplies: prepared Farm Animal Cards (page 32), premade tape of animal sounds, tape player, headphones

Setup: Obtain or make a tape of the sounds made by each animal featured on the Farm Animal Cards. There should be a long pause between each sound. Copy the Farm Animal Cards onto sturdy card stock. Color the cards with markers or crayons and cut them apart. Laminate the cards for durability. Place the cards and other supplies on a table in the center.

Directions: To play, a student should spread the nine cards faceup in front of her. Then, she should listen to the first animal sound on the tape. When she recognizes the sound, she should turn that animal's card facedown and wait for the next sound. Play continues until all nine cards are facedown.

Variation: Instead of using the tape, have a second player join the game. You will need two sets of Farm Animal Cards. One student spreads her cards in front of her as directed above. The second player holds the other stack in his lap. Player two should look at the top card and then make the sound of that animal for player one. Player one then turns the corresponding card facedown. Play continues until player one has turned all of her cards facedown. Have players switch roles and play again.

123 🐾 Measuring Feed

Supplies: large bowl of uncooked rice or dried beans; measuring cups and spoons; assortment of containers in various sizes; sensory table or large, shallow box (optional)

Setup: Fill the large bowl half full of uncooked rice or dried beans. Place the supplies on a table in the center. For easy cleanup, place the supplies in a sensory table or large, shallow box.

Directions: Explain to students that farmers have to feed and take care of their animals. (In this activity, students will use uncooked rice or dried beans to represent animal feed.) Have students use the measuring cups and spoons to measure the "feed" from the large bowl into the other various containers. Ask them to find out how many cups or spoonfuls it takes to fill each container. Also, have them determine how the cups relate to each other—how many 1/4 cups it takes to fill 1/2 cup, how many 1/3 cups it takes to fill 1 cup, etc.

♪ Farm Animal Singing

Supplies: Farm Animal Cards (page 32) glued to 9 plastic party hats, tape or CD of familiar children's songs, tape or CD player

Setup: Copy the Farm Animal Cards onto sturdy card stock. Color the cards with markers or crayons and cut them apart. Laminate the cards for durability. Glue each card onto the front of a party hat. Place the hats and other supplies on a table in the center.

Directions: Instruct each student to select a hat. Tell students that when the music is playing, they should sing the songs like the animals on the hats. For example, if a student has the cow hat, he should "moo" along with the songs. Students should switch hats periodically throughout a song or at the end of each song.

✋ Egg Poppers

Supplies: water table, water, plastic eggs (various sizes and colors)

Setup: Fill the water table half full of water. Place the eggs in the water.

Directions: Let students play with the eggs in the water. Suggest that they push the eggs under water and then let them "pop" to the surface. They can also move the eggs around by making small waves or open the eggs and fill and pour from them as desired.

Farm Animal Cards

Activities found on pages 30–31.

cow

horse

goose

chicken

sheep

goat

dog

cat

pig

Food

✍️✋ Punch Paint ....

Supplies: small cups or bowls of prepared punch paints; cotton swabs; paper; spoons; empty cups or bowls

Setup: Collect packets of powdered drink mixes in a variety of colors and flavors, such as lemonade, orange, strawberry, lime, and grape. Pour each packet of drink mix into a cup or bowl. Add approximately 1/3 cup of warm water to each and stir until the powder dissolves completely. Place the "punch paints" and other supplies on a table in the center.

Directions: Have students paint on the paper by dipping cotton swabs into the punch paints and using the swabs like paintbrushes. Encourage students to use as many different colors as they wish and to enjoy the scents as they paint.

Extension: Let students experiment with creating new punch paint colors by mixing together small amounts of two or more colors.

🎭 Let's Eat! ....

Supplies: small table and chairs, tablecloth, centerpiece, crayons, coloring sheets, menus, toy kitchen appliances, receipt book or small notebook, pencil, toy kitchen supplies (pots, pans, dishes, utensils, cups, plastic food, aprons, etc.), plastic storage container, towels, money manipulatives, toy cash register

Setup: Create a night on the town with a restaurant in the dramatic play center. Set up a small table and chairs complete with a tablecloth and centerpiece. Set another table aside for the host with crayons and coloring sheets for kids and restaurant menus. (These can be student created or teacher made.) Add a third station for the chef to make the food. Provide a receipt book and pencil for a server to take orders. You will also need supplies for a kitchen helper to clear the dishes into a plastic storage container and a place for washing dishes. Create another space where patrons can pay and leave a tip.

Directions: Explain the various areas of the center to students and help them select their roles. Then, let the playing begin!

◇ Library Literature ....

Bread and Jam for Frances by Russell Hoban (HarperTrophy, 1993)
Eating the Alphabet: Fruits and Vegetables from A to Z by Lois Ehlert
    (Voyager Books, 1993)
Food Fight! by Carol Diggory Shields (Handprint Books, 2002)
Gregory, the Terrible Eater by Mitchell Sharmat (Scholastic, 1989)
Mouse Mess by Linnea Riley (Scholastic, 1997)

👨‍🍳✋ Snack Mix Recipe ....

Supplies: bowls of bite-sized snack items, such as raisins, cheese crackers, dry cereal, dried fruits, nuts, etc.; small bowls; spoons; snack recipe cards

Setup: Fill each small bowl with a snack item. Put a spoon in each bowl. Prepare several snack recipes on large index cards. Glue three pieces of snack food to each card. (Or, draw illustrations of the foods.) Leave a space after each item. In the space, write a number from 1 to 3. Place the cards and other supplies on a table in the center.

Directions: Give each student a bowl and a snack recipe card. Using the card as a reference, the student should find the first item glued to the card, read the number, and place that number of spoonfuls of the item into her bowl. For example, if there is a *3* next to a raisin, then the student should scoop 3 spoonfuls of raisins into her bowl. Tell her to continue until all of the items on the card are in her bowl. Let students enjoy their snacks!

⌢ Egg Salad . . . .

Supplies: hard-boiled eggs, mayonnaise, mustard, pickle relish, crackers, plastic forks, bowls, spoons

Setup: Hard-boil the eggs in advance and refrigerate until cool. Place the supplies on a table in the center. (*Caution:* Raw or lightly cooked eggs may be contaminated with salmonella, a bacteria responsible for food poisoning. To prevent illness from bacteria, use only properly refrigerated, clean, sound-shelled, fresh, grade AA or A eggs; cook eggs until yolks are firm; and cook foods containing eggs thoroughly.)

Directions: Provide an illustrated recipe card with the following steps on it. Explain the steps to students as you demonstrate the activity. Each student should then follow the recipe.

1. Remove the shell from the egg.
2. Put the egg in your bowl and squish it with your fork.
3. Add 1 spoonful of mayonnaise and 1 spoonful of pickle relish to the bowl. Mix well.
4. Squirt 1 small dot of mustard into the egg mixture. Mix well.
5. Spoon your egg salad onto crackers and enjoy your snack!

123 Food Counting Booklets. . . . .

Supplies: Food Counting Booklet for each student, crayons, food stickers (or rubber stamps of foods and ink pads)

Setup: Prepare a booklet for each student by folding three pieces of paper in half. Staple along the fold to create a booklet. Help each student write *(Student's Name)'s Food Counting Booklet* on the cover.

Directions: Have each student open his booklet and use a crayon to number the pages from 1 to 10. Then, let him place the corresponding number of food stickers or stamps on each page. On the back cover of the booklet, tell him to write his favorite number and add the corresponding number of stickers or stamps.

▱ ✏ Yucky Foods . . . .

Supplies: lab books; pencils and crayons; ripe fruit, such as bananas, tomatoes, apples, oranges, and pears; resealable plastic bags; clear packing tape; permanent marker; magnifying glasses

Setup: At least one week before the center activity, prepare several bags as instructed in the directions below so that students can use them for comparison. Slice the fruit. Place the supplies on a table in the center.

Directions: Have each student select a type of fruit. Write the student's name and the name of the fruit on a resealable plastic bag with a permanent marker. Let the student place a few slices of the fruit in the bag. Help the student seal the bag tightly and cover the top with packing tape so that the bag cannot be opened again. Help the student tape the bag to a window or place it on a windowsill in the sun. Then, let students use magnifying glasses to examine the bags you prepared in advance. Have students predict what they think will happen to their bags over the next week and record their ideas and illustrations in their lab books. Help students watch and observe the bags over the next week.

✏ 🎨 🏠 My Favorite Recipe . . . .

Supplies: copies of the My Favorite Recipe Card Pattern (page 35); crayons or markers; pencils; toy food, cooking supplies, dishes, and utensils

Setup: Make a copy of the My Favorite Recipe Card Pattern for each student. Place the supplies on a table in the center.

Directions: Help each student write the instructions, including an ingredients list, for her favorite recipe on a copy of the My Favorite Recipe Card Pattern. Depending on students' writing abilities, you may need to write the recipes as they dictate to you. In the space provided, have each student illustrate the finished dish or part of the preparation process. Then, let students use the toy foods to prepare samples of their recipes.

Extension: Make copies of students' recipes and compile them into a class cookbook to place in the home living center.

My Favorite Recipe Card Pattern

Activity found on page 34.

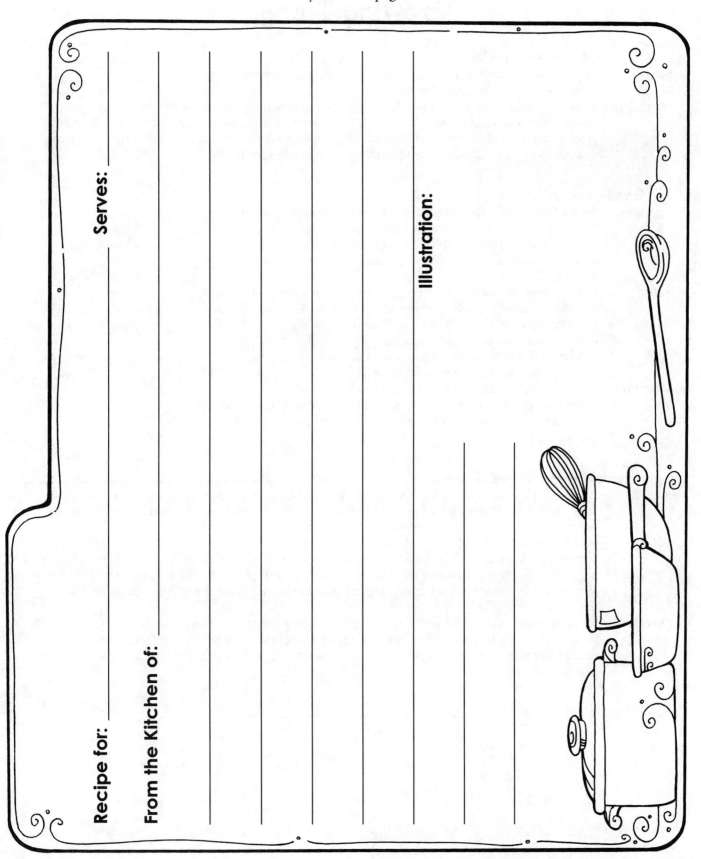

Recipe for: _____

From the Kitchen of: _____

Serves: _____

Illustration:

Growing Things

✎ 🖐 Mud Finger Painting . . . .

Supplies: dirt (not potting soil), bowls, water, spoons, construction paper
Setup: Place the supplies on a table in the center.
Directions: Have each student fill a bowl half full of dirt. Then, he should add a few spoonfuls of water and stir. Tell him to add more water as needed to create a pudding-like consistency. Students should then spoon some mud onto their construction paper and finger paint. Encourage them to create designs in the mud. Place the mud paintings in a sunny spot to dry.

🎭 Gardening . . . .

Supplies: plastic flowerpots, table, plastic or toy gardening tools, garden hose, toy wheelbarrow or wagon, small plastic fencing, seed packets, watering cans, artificial flowers, toy food, dustpan and broom, baskets, garden gloves, large bucket or trash can of newsprint "mulch"

Setup: Place a large tarp on the floor. Shred newsprint in a paper shredder to create "dirt" or "mulch" and put it in a large bucket or trash can. Create a table for potting flowers with empty plastic pots, artificial flowers, watering cans, seed packets, and plenty of "dirt." Create a vegetable garden by placing the toy food in rows on the tarp and covering them with the newsprint dirt.
Directions: Help students choose roles and begin playing in the garden. Encourage students to dig up the vegetables, pretend to plant more seeds, and water them with the hose while others plant flowers in the flowerpots.

🧤 ✎ Flower Necklaces . . . .

Supplies: bowl of 1" (2.5 cm) flower shapes cut from construction paper or sheets of foam (tip: most craft stores sell flower-shaped punches or precut foam shapes), yarn, wooden beads (1 per student), bowl of pieces of plastic drinking straws, bowl of fruit-flavored cereal rings
Setup: Punch a hole in the center of each flower shape and put it in a bowl. Cut an 18" (46 cm) piece of yarn for each student. Tie a wooden bead onto one end of each piece of yarn. Wrap a piece of masking tape around the other end for easy threading. Cut plastic drinking straws into 1" (2.5 cm) lengths. Place the straws and cereal rings in separate bowls. Place the supplies on a table in the center.
Directions: Allow students to string flowers, cereal rings, and straw pieces onto their pieces of yarn as desired. When a necklace has been filled to a student's satisfaction, tie the ends together and slip it over the student's head. Encourage students to use patterning skills while stringing the flowers, straws, and cereal.

◇ Library Literature . . . .

The Carrot Seed by Ruth Krauss (HarperTrophy, 2004)
From Seed to Plant by Gail Gibbons (Holiday House, 1993)
Growing Vegetable Soup by Lois Ehlert (Voyager Books, 1990)
How Do Apples Grow? by Betsy Maestro (HarperTrophy, 1993)
Planting a Rainbow by Lois Ehlert (Voyager Books, 1992)

🖐 Seed Shakers..

Supplies: small envelopes; bowls of different sizes of seeds, such as grass, corn, beans, flowers, etc.; empty seed packets; crayons or markers

Setup: Pour each type of seed into a bowl. Keep the empty seed packets with the corresponding bowls so that students can identify each type of seed. Place the supplies on a table in the center.

Directions: Give each student two envelopes to decorate with pictures of his favorite growing things. Next, have him choose two different kinds of seeds, pinch a small amount of each, and place them in his two separate envelopes. Help him tightly seal the envelopes. Then, tell students to shake their envelopes to hear the differences in the sounds.

Extension: Prepare two envelopes of each type of seed. Seal the envelopes and place them on a table in the center. Encourage students to try to match the envelopes by listening to the sounds they make when they are shaken.

123 🖐 Seed Cards..

Supplies: bowls of large seeds, such as corn, beans, peas, etc.; index cards; crayons or markers; glue

Setup: Pour each type of seed into a bowl. Place the bowls and other supplies on a table in the center.

Directions: Give each student an index card. Have her choose a number from 1 to 10 and write it on the card. Then, tell her to glue that number of seeds onto her card. She can use the same type of seed or mix and match as she wishes. Let students continue making seed cards as long as time and interest allows. You may want to encourage them to each make a set of seed cards for numbers from 1 to 10.

🖐 ✏ Growing Seeds..

Supplies: lab books; pencils and crayons; foil pie pans; potting soil; spoons; sturdy card stock stencils; fast-growing grass seeds, such as rye; small watering can

Setup: Cut several stencils of familiar and popular shapes, such as butterflies, bugs, cars, geometric shapes, etc., out of sturdy card stock. (Or, use premade stencils.) Write each student's name on the bottom of a pie pan with a permanent marker. Place the stencils and other supplies on a table in the center.

Directions: Instruct students to fill their pie pans with potting soil and add a little water. Tell them to stir the mixture and spread it in the pan. Then, let each student choose a stencil and place it over his pan. Each student should use a spoon or his fingers to sprinkle seeds over the dirt through the opening in the stencil. Help students carefully remove the stencils so that extra seeds do not get planted outside of the shaped areas. Place the pie pans in a sunny location and let students water them as needed. Have students write and draw their predictions in their lab books and monitor their seeds' progress for the next two weeks.

🖐 Worms & Dirt..

Supplies: sensory table filled with dirt, gravel, and sand; rubber fishing worms (without hooks); measuring cups; sifters; slotted spoons

Setup: Fill a sensory table with dirt, gravel, and sand. Mix them together, or separate them into sections. Bury several worms in the dirt, gravel, and sand. Place the other supplies on top of the mixture.

Directions: Allow students to sift through the table using their bare hands and the cups and sifters. Encourage them to talk about what they see, hear, smell, and feel as they explore in the sensory table.

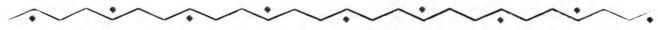

Holidays

Halloween

🎨 Decoupage Pumpkins. . . . .

Supplies: small baking pumpkins, bowls of colorful tissue paper squares, bowl of glue or liquid starch, foam paintbrushes, plastic foam plates

Setup: Write each student's name on the stem of a pumpkin with a permanent marker. Cut the tissue paper into approximately 1" (2.5 cm) squares. Sort the squares by color and place each color in a different bowl. Thin glue or liquid starch with water and pour it into a bowl. Place all of the supplies on a table in the center.

Directions: Have each student find the pumpkin with her name on it and place it on a plate. Let each student use a foam paintbrush to apply glue to a small section of the pumpkin. Then, she should stick two or three squares of tissue paper to the glue. Tell her to continue this process until the entire pumpkin is covered in tissue paper. Encourage students to overlap the tissue paper squares to create a colorful stained-glass effect. When the pumpkin is covered, each student should paint a layer of glue over the entire surface to saturate all of the tissue paper. Leave the pumpkins on the plates to dry.

🎭 Trick-or-Treating. . . . .

Supplies: Halloween costumes, plastic pumpkin pails or candy bags, appliance box "houses," bowls of wrapped candy or small manipulatives

Setup: Create a neighborhood by decorating the appliance boxes to represent houses. If desired, let students help. Place a small amount of wrapped candy (or manipulatives if you prefer) in a bowl inside each "house."

Directions: Let some students pretend to be home owners and some pretend to be trick-or-treaters. Have the trick-or-treaters dress up in Halloween costumes while the home owners crawl into the houses to distribute candy. As trick-or-treaters approach each house, they should knock and say, "Trick or treat." Remind students to thank the home owners after they are given candy. Have students trade places so that everyone gets a chance to trick-or-treat.

◇ Library Literature . . . .

Big Pumpkin by Erica Silverman (Aladdin, 1995)
Inside a House That Is Haunted: A Rebus Read-Along Story by Alyssa Satin Capucilli (Scholastic, 1998)
It's Pumpkin Time! by Zoe Hall (Scholastic Paperbacks, 1999)
The Little Old Lady Who Was Not Afraid of Anything by Linda Williams (HarperTrophy, 1988)
Too Many Pumpkins by Linda White (Holiday House, 1997)

123 🕷 Guess & Count

Supplies: 6 types of small Halloween objects, such as wrapped candy, plastic spider rings and other novelty items, etc.; 6 clear plastic jars with lids, labeled from 1 to 6; paper; crayons

Setup: Make six labels, each with a number from 1 to 6. Place the labels on the jars. Put a different number of items in each jar. Do not include more items than students can count; the jars do not need to be full. Put the lids on the jars. Place the jars and other supplies on a table in the center.

Directions: Help each student write his name and numbers from 1 to 6 on a piece of paper. Then, tell him to examine each jar from all sides and guess how many items are in it. He should write his guess next to the corresponding number on his paper. After each student has written his guess for all six jars, he should open a jar and count the items inside. Tell him to write the actual number beside his original guess, using a different color crayon. Have students place the items back inside the jars and close the lids before opening another jar. Finally, encourage students to look at the differences between the numbers they guessed and the actual number of objects in each jar.

♪ Making Spooky Music

Supplies: tape recorder; cassette tape; musical instruments; items that can be used as instruments, such as foil pie pans, empty paper towel tubes, empty coffee cans, etc.

Setup: Place the supplies on a table in the center.

Directions: Demonstrate the musical instruments and other noise-making objects for students and encourage them to make their own spooky sounds. Prompt students with questions, such as, "What does the wind sound like when it howls?" or, "What do you think creaky doors or rattling windows sound like?" Have students experiment with the instruments and noisemakers. When they are ready, help them record their spooky music with the tape recorder. Let them rewind the tape and replay their spooky music.

🍃 ✏ Comparing Pumpkins

Supplies: lab books, pencils and crayons, variety of small to medium pumpkins (students should be able to easily lift each pumpkin), scale, fabric measuring tape

Setup: Choose pumpkins that vary in size, weight, shape, color, and texture. Place the supplies on a table in the center.

Directions: Encourage students to compare the pumpkins and record their findings in their lab books. Have them estimate the pumpkins' weights by lifting them and then find the actual weights using the scale. Ask them if they think size is related to weight. Show students how to use the measuring tape to find the circumference of each pumpkin. They can also compare the pumpkins by feeling the skin textures or thumping them. Have students classify and group the pumpkins by various characteristics.

✋ 🕷 What's Inside?

Supplies: pumpkins; scooping tools, such as spoons, ice cream scoops, measuring cups, etc.

Setup: Use a sharp knife to cut the tops off the pumpkins. Place the pumpkins and scooping tools on a newspaper-covered table in the center.

Directions: Prepare students for a messy experience! Encourage students to put their hands inside the pumpkins. Invite them to enjoy manipulating the pulp and the seeds with their hands and the scooping tools. Have them explore each pumpkin separately to see which one has the thickest rind, the most seeds, the slimiest pulp, etc.

Thanksgiving

🎨 Hand Painted Turkeys ....

Supplies: copies of the Turkey Pattern (page 42) on brown construction paper or card stock, glue, large pieces of white paper, several colors of tempera paint in foil pie pans

Setup: Make a copy and cut out the Turkey Pattern without the feet. Trace the pattern onto brown construction paper for each student. Or, copy the pattern onto brown card stock. Cut out the turkeys. Pour a thin layer of each paint color in the bottom of a pie pan. Place the supplies on a table in the center.

Directions: Help students glue the Turkey Patterns onto white paper. Then, let each student press one palm into a pan of paint. Instruct her to press her two palms together to spread the paint to the tips of her fingers and then make handprints on her paper to create turkey feathers. After she washes her hands, let her choose another color and continue creating feathers. To make feet for the turkey, have her dip her palms into orange paint and spread the paint to the tips of her fingers. Then, she should hold her fingers close together with the thumbs extended to make prints on her paper. Finally, she should add eyes by making two fingerprints with dark paint.

🎭 🏠 Thanksgiving Village ....

Supplies: empty appliance boxes, cardboard tubes (from wrapping paper or paper towels), table and chairs, broom, artificial rocks, firewood, large plastic kettle, toy food and dishes, ornamental corn and gourds, five 6' (2 m) pieces of 1" (2.5 cm) plastic plumbing pipe, rope, large blankets, traditional Native American headdresses and pilgrim hats (premade or teacher made from construction paper)

Setup: Help students "construct" a village for celebrating the first Thanksgiving. Make "log houses" by gluing cardboard tubes to appliance boxes or paint logs on the boxes. To build a tepee, arrange the plastic pipes so that they are standing in a cone shape. Tie them together at the top with rope. Wrap a blanket around the outside of the pipes and tie it in place at the top and bottom. Build a "fire" using the firewood surrounded by a ring of rocks. Place the kettle on top of the wood. Set up a table and chairs for the dinner. Place the food and dishes inside the log house and tepee so that the food can be brought to the dinner table.

Directions: Encourage students playing in the center to create a Thanksgiving feast for everyone in the "village." Also, remind students that they will need to take care of their village by feeding the fire, sweeping the camp, cooking over the fire, setting the table, washing dishes, gathering food, etc.

👟 🪶 Turkey Tag ....

Supplies: large feathers (available at most craft stores)

Setup: Place the supplies on a table in the center. (*Caution:* Before completing any feather activity, inquire about students' allergies.) This activity requires space to run. It is an excellent game to play outside.

Directions: Help each student place a feather in his back pocket or waistband. Tell students to try to capture classmates' tail feathers without having their own feathers captured. When a student's feather is pulled, it should be returned immediately to the student and play continues.

✋ Mayflower Soap Boats ....

Supplies: sensory table, several floating bath soap boats

Setup: Cut several rectangles out of construction paper or card stock. They should be about the same size as a bar of soap. Tape a toothpick to each rectangle to make a sail for a "boat." Press each toothpick into a bar of soap to make a boat. Fill the sensory table with water.

Directions: Let students carefully float the soap boats in the water. Tell them to try not to get the sails wet. Encourage students to blow gently on the sails to push the boats across the water. Have them count how many times they have to blow to move a boat from one side of the table to the other.

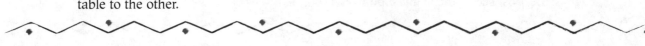

◇ **Library Literature** ....

10 Fat Turkeys by Tony Johnston (Cartwheel, 2004)
Thanksgiving Is for Giving Thanks by Margaret Sutherland (Grosset & Dunlap, 2000)
A Turkey for Thanksgiving by Eve Bunting (Clarion Books, 1995)
Turkey Surprise by Peggy Archer (Dial, 2005)
'Twas the Night Before Thanksgiving by Dav Pilkey (Scholastic Paperbacks, 2004)

123 🔍 **Turkey Feather Count** ....

Supplies: 10 copies of the Turkey Pattern (page 42), each glued to a piece of plastic foam ball; stiff feathers
(available at most craft stores)

Setup: Write numbers from 1 to 10 on the Turkey
Patterns. Color as desired and cut out the
turkeys. Fold each turkey so that its feet and
the bottom fourth of its body are resting on the
table. (See illustration.) Cut 5 plastic foam balls,
approximately 6" (15 cm) diameter, in half.
Cut off a slice at the bottom of each foam half
sphere to create a flat base. Glue each turkey
to a plastic foam piece. Each turkey will now sit
up. Arrange the 10 turkeys in random order on
a table in the center. Place the feathers on the
table, as well. (*Caution:* Before completing any
feather activity, inquire about students' allergies.)

Directions: Have each student read the number on a turkey and insert that number of "tail feathers" into the
plastic foam. When he has added the correct number of tail feathers for all of the turkeys, have
him remove them so that the next player can take a turn.

Variation: Instead of writing numbers on the turkeys, write simple math sentences for students to solve. Have
them insert the number of feathers that corresponds to each answer. Or, draw color patterns for
students to match and repeat with colorful feathers.

♪ 🎨 **Native American Drums** ....

Supplies: undecorated coffee can drums, feathers, sequins, crayons or markers, glue

Setup: For each drum, cut off the neck of a large balloon and stretch the top portion of the balloon tightly
over the open end of a lidless coffee can. Secure the balloon in place with duct tape. Cut brown
craft paper or paper grocery bags into rectangles that will wrap around empty coffee cans. Glue a
piece of craft paper around the drum. Place the drums and other supplies on a table in the center.

Directions: Have each student decorate a drum using crayons, markers, feathers, and sequins. Encourage
students to use repeating patterns and geometric shapes in their decorations. Let the glue dry.
When the drums are dry, tell students to play rhythms by tapping the drums with their hands.
Suggest experimenting with how to make different sounds by tapping on the sides of the drums,
using their fingers or palms, etc.

✏ 🎨 **Thankful Turkey** ....

Supplies: 1 copy of a "Thankful Turkey" for each student, colorful construction paper feathers, glue, crayons

Setup: Write *I am thankful.* on the body of a copy of the Turkey Pattern (page 42). Make a copy for
each student in the class. Cut feathers, each approximately 4"–5" (10 cm–13 cm) long, out of
construction paper. Place the supplies on a table in the center.

Directions: Have each student choose several feathers and write or dictate the things she is thankful for. Help
her write each thing on a feather. Then, let each student color and cut out her turkey. Finally, help
each student arrange her tail feathers and glue them to her turkey.

Turkey Pattern

Activities found on pages 40–41.

 CD-104198 *It's Center Time!*

HanukKah

🖐123 Star of David: Lacing Activity ....

Supplies: Star of David lacing board

Setup: Use a ruler and marker to draw a 9" (23 cm) square on a piece of poster board. Cut out the square. Using a ruler and marker, mark the center of the top and bottom edges of the square. On the left and right edges, divide the lengths into thirds and mark 1/3 and 2/3. On all four sides, punch two holes side-by-side at each mark, approximately 1" (2.5 cm) from the edges of the square. (See illustration.) Number the holes as shown. If desired, draw dotted lines to connect the holes on the board for students to use as guides. Tie the end of a piece of yarn that is approximately 5' (1.5 m) long through the hole labeled *1*. Wrap a small piece of masking tape around the other end of the yarn for easier threading. Place the lacing board on a table in the center.

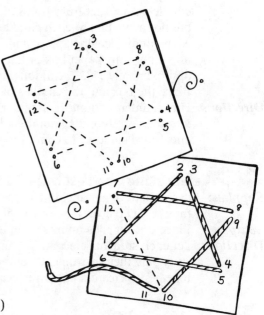

Directions: Have students lace the yarn through the holes in numerical order to create a Star of David. They should pass the yarn down through one hole and up through the second hole so that the star pattern will be visible on top of the lacing board. (See illustration.)

🍪 Decorating Cookies ....

Supplies: rolls of sugar cookie dough, rolling pins, all-purpose flour, Hanukkah cookie cutters, colorful frosting, tubes of decorating frosting, cookie-decorating candies, sprinkles, paper plates, plastic knives

Setup: Prepare a table in the center by spreading flour for the dough. Open the rolls of dough. Place the supplies on a table in the center. You will bake the cookies for students. Keep students away from all hot surfaces. If you do not have access to an oven at school, bake the cookies in advance and have students decorate them or purchase premade shaped cookies for students to decorate.

Directions: Provide an illustrated recipe card with the following steps on it. Explain the steps to students as you demonstrate the activity. Each student should then follow the recipe.

1. Roll out the dough and cut out shapes with the cookie cutters.
2. Place the cookies on a baking sheet. (An adult will bake the cookies for you.)
3. When cookies are cool, spread frosting on them with a plastic knife.
4. Decorate the cookies with candy, tubes of frosting, and sprinkles.
5. Enjoy your snack!

◇ Library Literature ....

Biscuit's Hanukkah by Alyssa Satin Capucilli (HarperFestival, 2005)
The Chanukkah Guest by Eric A. Kimmel (Holiday House, 1992)
Hanukkah! by Roni Schotter (Megan Tingley, 1993)
Sammy Spider's First Hanukkah by Sylvia A. Rouss (Kar-Ben Publishing, 1993)
What Is Hanukkah? by Harriet Ziefert (Festival, 1994)

123 Counting Menorah Candles

Supplies: craft stick candles, prepared "Menorah" box

Setup: Cut eight strips of colorful construction paper, each approximately 5" x 2" (12.5 cm x 5 cm). Cut out eight construction paper "flames" to glue to the tops of the strips to make construction paper candles. Add a set from 1 to 8 of small Hanukkah stickers (or star stickers if Hanukkah stickers are not available) to each candle. Laminate them for durability. Glue a craft stick to the back of each candle, leaving approximately 2" (5 cm) of the stick below the base of the candle. Wrap an empty copy paper box or large shoe box with wrapping paper. Carefully cut eight slits, each approximately 1" (2.5 cm) long, in a row across the top of the box. Label the slits from 1 to 8. Place the box and the candles on a table in the center.

Directions: Have students count the number of stickers on each candle and insert the end of the craft stick into the corresponding numbered slit on the box. When all eight of the candles are in place, encourage students to count the menorah candles aloud.

♪ 👟 Celebrating the Festival of Lights

Supplies: assortment of handheld percussion instruments, such as tambourines, triangles, and hand drums; tape or CD player; tape or CD of popular and traditional Hanukkah songs

Setup: Place the supplies on a table in the center.

Directions: Let each student select an instrument. Help students turn on the music and encourage them to sing, play their instruments, and dance along to the music. For a challenge, have students work together to create a pattern to play along with the music.

🍃 ✏️ Magical Oil

Supplies: lab books; pencils and crayons; variety of items that produce light, such as a lamp, a flashlight, a candle, a glow stick, an oil lamp, and a candle; cooking oil; plastic plate; variety of absorbent and nonabsorbent items, such as paper towels, socks, copy paper, aluminum foil, waxed paper, etc.

Setup: Place the supplies on a table in the center.

Directions: Before beginning the activity, discuss the different ways that the items create light. Let students examine each item. (Do not actually light candles or the oil lamp.) Talk to students about the oil lamp and how it works by soaking the wick in the oil and burning slowly. Tell students that they will be trying to decide which materials make the best wicks. Pour a small amount of oil onto the plate. Touch the corner of a paper towel to the oil and have students draw pictures in their lab books of what happens. Then, let students experiment with the other items to decide which are absorbent and which are not. Remind them to record their findings in their lab books. Ask them to write about or draw pictures of the material that makes the best wick.

✏️ 🎨 Hanukkah Greeting Cards

Supplies: construction paper strips; tissue paper squares; folded construction paper cards; glue; markers; crayons; card decorating supplies, such as glitter, stickers, and decorative hole punches

Setup: Cut eight strips of colorful construction paper, each approximately 1/2" x 3" (1.25 cm x 7.5 cm), for each student. Cut yellow, red, and orange tissue paper into small squares, approximately 3" x 3" (7.5 cm x 7.5 cm). Fold the construction paper in half to prepare cards for students. Place the supplies on a table in the center.

Directions: Have each student glue eight "candles" in a row on the front of her card. Let students use tissue paper squares to make a "flame" for each candle by wrinkling a few squares into a ball and gluing the ball to the top of a candle. Let students decorate their cards as they wish. When the glue is dry, help them write messages on their cards. On the fronts of the cards, students may wish to write words, such as *Hanukkah*, *Love*, *Lights*, or their names, by placing one letter on each candle. Let students dictate messages to write inside the cards and then present them to family or friends.

Christmas

🎭 Santa's Workshop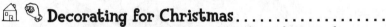

Supplies: toys, paintbrushes, toy tools, table and chairs, aprons, elf hats (purchased or teacher made from construction paper), boxes, ribbons, bows, wagon, large Christmas stockings, large duffel bag, Santa hat and coat, small pillow, reindeer antler headband

Setup: Create Santa's workshop in the dramatic play center. Provide a table and chairs for elves to make and paint toys. Provide a second area for putting toys in boxes and tying with bows. Turn a wagon into Santa's sleigh that will be pulled by a "reindeer." The small pillow will be used to give Santa a big belly.

Directions: Help students select the roles they will play in Santa's workshop. Encourage students to "build" toys, wrap them, load all of the gifts into Santa's duffel bag, put it on the sleigh, and help Santa deliver the gifts by placing them in the stockings.

🏠 🖐 Decorating for Christmas

Supplies: artificial Christmas tree; large box of assorted decorations, such as wreaths, tinsel, garland, ornaments, stockings, etc.; small toys from the classroom; boxes; wrapping paper; clear tape; bows; gift tags

Setup: Place a large box of Christmas decorations in the home living center. Set up the Christmas tree. Create a gift-wrapping station on a table in the center.

Directions: Encourage students to decorate the home center for the holiday. Let them decorate the tree, string tinsel or garland around the center, and wrap "gifts" (small classroom toys) for their classmates and place them under the tree.

👨‍🍳 Christmas Cookies

Supplies: rolls of sugar cookie dough, rolling pins, all-purpose flour, Christmas cookie cutters, colorful frosting, tubes of decorating frosting, cookie-decorating candies, sprinkles, paper plates, plastic knives

Setup: Prepare a table in the center by spreading flour for the dough. Open the rolls of dough. Place the supplies on a table in the center. You will bake the cookies for students. Keep students away from all hot surfaces. If you do not have access to an oven at school, bake the cookies in advance and have students decorate them or purchase premade shaped cookies for students to decorate.

Directions: Provide an illustrated recipe card with the following steps on it. Explain the steps to students as you demonstrate the activity. Each student should then follow the recipe.
1. Roll out the dough and cut out shapes with the cookie cutters.
2. Place the cookies on a baking sheet. (An adult will bake the cookies for you.)
3. When cookies are cool, spread frosting on them with a plastic knife.
4. Decorate the cookies with candy, tubes of frosting, and sprinkles.
5. Enjoy your snack!

🔷 Library Literature

Bear Stays Up for Christmas by Karma Wilson (Scholastic, 2005)
Merry Christmas Mom and Dad by Mercer Mayer (Golden Books, 1999)
On Christmas Eve by Margaret Wise Brown (HarperTrophy, 2000)
The Polar Express by Chris Van Allsburg (Houghton Mifflin, 1985)
The Sweet Smell of Christmas by Patricia M. Scarry (Golden Books, 2003)

123 Christmas Countdown

Supplies: December calendar for each student, Christmas stickers, crayons or markers

Setup: On a piece of white copy paper, make a calendar grid for the month of December. Leave a blank border area around the calendar for students to decorate. Make a copy of the calendar on red or green paper for each student. Place the calendars and other supplies on a table in the center.

Directions: Let each student decorate his calendar using stickers and crayons or markers. As each day of December passes, have students cross out the corresponding squares on the calendars. Or, let students take their calendars home and use them to count down the days with their families.

Rockin' Jingle Bells

Supplies: assortment of jingle bells, chenille stems, tape or CD player, tape or CD of jazzy Christmas songs

Setup: Place the supplies on a table in the center.

Directions: Let each student string a few jingle bells onto a chenille stem and twist the ends together to make a circle. Help students turn on the music and encourage them to sing, ring their jingle bells, and dance along to the music. For even more fun, have students try to ring two or more sets of jingle bells at once.

Smells of Christmas

Supplies: prepared cups with scented items inside; bowls

Setup: Decorate empty, clean yogurt cups as desired. Use a nail to punch three holes in the lids of the cups. Collect a variety of scented items that remind people of Christmas, such as fresh pinecones, cinnamon, oranges, peppermint, hot chocolate mix, vanilla spices, etc. Put a small amount of each scented item in a yogurt cup and secure the lid in place with tape. Put a small amount of each item in a bowl. Place the cups and bowls on a table in the center.

Directions: Have each student smell an item through the holes in a yogurt cup and then find the matching scent in one of the bowls. Let students match all of the scents.

What Can I Give To You?

Supplies: colorful construction paper with a large square drawn on each piece, crayons, markers, gift bows, gift tags (or tags cut from construction paper), glue

Setup: Draw a large square on a piece of construction paper for each student. Place the supplies on a table in the center.

Directions: Encourage each student to think of a gift that she would like to give to someone in her family. Remind students that gifts do not have to be material objects; sometimes a big hug or a kind deed can be the greatest gift of all! Have each student draw a picture of the gift in the box on her construction paper. Below the box, have her write or dictate about the gift and why she wants to give it to the recipient. Let each student write the recipient's name on a gift tag and glue the tag and a bow to the top of the square to complete her gift.

Valentine's Day

🎨 Heart Collage Paintings . . . .

Supplies: large pieces of white construction paper; construction paper hearts; red, purple, and pink tempera paint in foil pie pans; cotton balls; removable sticky tack or glue sticks

Setup: Cut out several hearts in different sizes from construction paper. Pour a thin layer of paint into each pie pan. Place the supplies on a table in the center.

Directions: Give each student a piece of white construction paper. Tell him to select a heart cutout and apply a small piece of sticky tack or a small stripe of glue to the back of the heart. Have him temporarily stick the heart somewhere on his white paper. Then, each student should dip a cotton ball into one of the pans of paint and brush from the middle of the heart onto the white construction paper. He should brush all of the way around the heart in this manner. Then, instruct him to remove the heart and discard it. A white heart surrounded by brushed paint will remain on his paper. Let students continue placing hearts on their papers and painting around them with various colors. Encourage students to experiment with overlapping hearts, different sized hearts, various brush strokes and patterns, etc. Set aside the papers to dry.

🎭 🖌 Valentine Factory . . . .

Supplies: colorful construction paper; hole punch; valentine-making supplies, such as crayons, markers, sequins, ribbon, doilies, glue, etc.; envelopes; "cupid hats"; construction paper hearts; toy ride-on car; canvas shoulder bag; 10 storage bins or shoe boxes

Setup: Cut out a large supply of hearts from construction paper. Make "cupid hats" for the factory workers by stapling heart cutouts to headbands of construction paper. Establish a "time clock" area where workers will "punch in and out" when entering and leaving the factory. Write each student's name on a paper heart and put it in a box or envelope at the entrance to the center. Place the hole punch near the box or envelope. Set up an assembly table in the "factory" with all of the valentine-making supplies in an assembly line. Create a delivery vehicle by decorating the toy ride-on car with hearts. Number the bins or shoe boxes from 1 to 10 and place them around the perimeter of the center to represent 10 neighborhood mailboxes.

Directions: When students enter the center, they should find their hearts and "punch in" with the hole punch. Then, they should put on their cupid hats and begin assembling valentines! Encourage students to put the valentines in envelopes and write a number from 1 to 10 on each envelope. When a batch is complete, a student should act as the delivery person and put the valentines in the canvas bag. She should drive from one mailbox to another to deliver the numbered valentines to the corresponding mailboxes. Have students take turns so that everyone gets a chance to be the delivery person.

👟 🎵 Heart Jump . . . .

Supplies: tape or CD player; tape or CD of energetic music

Setup: Cut large hearts out of paper or poster board. The hearts can all be the same size or various sizes. Laminate the hearts for durability and use clear packing tape to secure them to the floor in a large center area. Place the supplies on a table in the center.

Directions: Play music while students jump from heart to heart. Encourage them to try skipping from heart to heart, jumping sideways, jumping backward, and hopping on one foot.

🧑‍🍳 Chocolate-Dipped Fruit.....................................

Supplies: whole strawberries with stems, bananas, bowl of dipping chocolate, paper plates, resealable plastic bags

Setup: Wash the strawberries and slice the bananas into 2" (5 cm) pieces. Put the chocolate in a bowl and melt it in the microwave. (Allow it to cool enough to avoid burns before students begin the activity.) Place the supplies on a table in the center.

Directions: Provide an illustrated recipe card with the following steps on it. Explain the steps to students as you demonstrate the activity. Each student should then follow the recipe.

1. Hold a strawberry by its stem or one end of a piece of banana and dip it halfway into the bowl of chocolate.
2. Place the chocolate-dipped fruit on a plate to cool.
3. Make 2 more chocolate treats to share with a friend or family member.
4. Place 2 treats in a resealable plastic bag and enjoy the third treat as a snack!

◇ Library Literature...

The Day It Rained Hearts by Felicia Bond (HarperTrophy, 2006)
Froggy's First Kiss by Jonathan London (Puffin, 1999)
It's Valentine's Day by Jack Prelutsky (HarperTrophy, 1996)
The Night Before Valentine's Day by Natasha Wing (Grosset & Dunlap, 2001)
Roses Are Pink, Your Feet Really Stink by Diane deGroat (HarperTrophy, 1997)

123 Sequencing Hearts..

Supplies: strips of construction paper, bowls of construction paper hearts, glue sticks

Setup: Cut several long strips of construction paper that are each approximately 3" (7.5 cm) wide. Cut out three hearts of different sizes. Use the three hearts as templates and cut out several of each size. Put the three different sized hearts into three different bowls. Place the bowls and other supplies on a table in the center.

Directions: Give each student a long strip of paper. Have her select two hearts from each container and arrange the hearts in order from smallest to largest. Then, have each student glue the hearts to the strip of paper.

Extension: Have each student take 10 hearts of the same size. Help her number the hearts from 1 to 10. Let her shuffle the hearts and arrange them in order on her paper strip. Have her glue them to the strip of paper in the correct order when she is finished arranging them.

✏️ 🎨 Making Cards..

Supplies: construction paper; card-decorating supplies, such as crayons, markers, decorative punches, stickers, doilies, glitter, sequins, glue sticks, etc.; envelopes

Setup: Fold several sheets of construction paper to make cards. Place the supplies on a table in the center.

Directions: Help students practice using words to communicate. Let them create valentines for important people in their lives. Encourage students to write or dictate at least one or two sentences for each card. Then, have them decorate the cards using the supplies. Let students place the completed cards in envelopes and deliver them to the recipients.

Insects

Rainbow Honeycombs

Supplies: Hexagon Patterns (page 51) copied onto colorful copy paper, paper plates, scissors, glue sticks, copies of honeybee clip art (optional), crayons or markers (optional)

Setup: Copy the Hexagon Patterns onto several sheets of colorful copy paper. Cut out seven hexagons to use to demonstrate the activity for students. If you choose to use clip art, make several copies of the honeybee clip art on white paper. Place the copies and other supplies on a table in the center.

Directions: Encourage students to practice their scissors skills while creating rainbow honeycombs! Using the hexagons that you cut out, show students how the shapes fit together to look like a honeycomb. Then, have each student select several pieces of colorful paper with hexagons on them. Each student should cut out one or two hexagons in each color. Each student will need seven hexagons to complete the project. When all of the hexagons are cut out, tell each student to arrange them on her plate and glue them in place. Finally, provide copies of the honeybee clip art for students to color, cut out, and glue onto the honeycombs (optional).

Web Weaving

Supplies: paper or plastic foam plates, colorful yarn, tape, insect and spider stickers

Setup: Use scissors to cut 1" (2.5 cm) slits, spaced approximately 2" (5 cm) apart, around the perimeter of each plate. Cut the yarn into pieces, each approximately 1 yd. (1 m) in length. Place all of the supplies on a table in the center.

Directions: Have each student choose a piece of yarn and tape one end to the back of his plate. Then, tell him to weave the yarn in a random pattern by wrapping it around the plate and through the precut slits. Remind students not to pull the yarn too tightly or the plates will fold. When he reaches the end of a piece of yarn, have him tape the end to the back of the plate and select another piece of yarn. Let him continue until he has created a yarn web on his plate. Encourage students to place the insect and spider stickers on their webs.

Don't Get Caught in the Web!

Supplies: web obstacle course

Setup: Arrange large, sturdy obstacles, such as chairs, tables, and bookcases, around the perimeter of the center area. Tie one end of a skein of yarn around a chair or table leg. Weave a "web" of yarn around the play area, anchoring it to chairs, tables, and bookcases by tying it or using tape. Keep the web at students' knee-level. Don't weave too much yarn into the web; students should be able to step into the openings between the lengths of yarn.

Directions: Tell students to pretend they are flying insects trying not to get caught in a spider's web. Encourage them to cross from one side of the play area to the other without touching the web. They can crawl under the web or step carefully through it.

Library Literature

Crickwing by Janell Cannon (Voyager Books, 2005)
The Grouchy Ladybug by Eric Carle (HarperTrophy, 1996)
The Icky Bug Counting Book by Jerry Pallotta (Charlesbridge Publishing, 1992)
Old Black Fly by Jim Aylesworth (Henry Holt and Co., 1995)
The Very Hungry Caterpillar by Eric Carle (Philomel, 1994)

Ladybug Apples . . . .

Supplies: red apples, pretzel sticks, peanut butter or cream cheese, raisins, paper or plastic foam plates, plastic spoons or knives

Setup: Cut the apples in half and remove the cores. Use a wooden skewer to punch holes for six legs and two antennae in each apple half. (See illustration for placement.) If desired, students can help you with this step. Place all of the supplies on a table in the center.

Directions: Provide an illustrated recipe card with the following steps on it. Explain the steps to students as you demonstrate the activity. Each student should then follow the recipe.

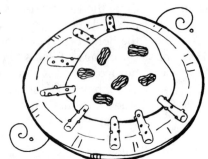

1. Place your apple half on a plate with the red side up.
2. Count out 8 pretzel sticks. Put them in the holes to make legs and antennae.
3. Stick raisins to the apple using peanut butter or cream cheese.
4. Count the spots on your ladybug before you enjoy your snack.

Spots on a Ladybug . . . .

Supplies: copies of the Ladybug Pattern (page 52), crayons or markers, ink pad with black washable ink

Setup: Make a copy of the Ladybug Pattern for each student. Place the supplies on a table in the center.

Directions: Have each student use the ink pad to make thumbprints on her ladybug's back. When she is finished, let her use crayons or markers to draw six legs and two antennae on her ladybug. She may also color the ladybug if she chooses. Have students count the spots, legs, and antennae aloud and write these numbers on their papers.

Extension: Reduce the Ladybug Pattern and make 10 copies. Color the ladybugs, cut them out, and glue them to index cards. Draw black spots on each ladybug to create sets of 1 to 10. On a separate set of cards, write numbers from 1 to 10. Laminate the cards for durability. Place all of the cards in the center. Have students match the ladybug cards to the number cards.

 Flight of the Bumblebee . . . .

Supplies: bumblebee finger puppets, tape or CD player, tape or CD of "The Flight of the Bumblebee" from *The Tale of Tsar Saltan* by Nikolay Andreyevich Rimsky-Korsakov

Setup: Create a bumblebee finger puppet for each student. Cut chenille stems in half. Cut out 3" x 2" (7.5 cm x 5 cm) rectangles from tissue paper. Create "wings" by pinching each tissue paper rectangle in the middle. Twist the end of a piece of chenille stem around the middle of the wings. Make a finger-sized loop in the other end of the stem. Place the puppets and supplies on a table in the center.

Directions: Have each student put on a bumblebee finger puppet. Start the music and let students move their puppets and bodies to the rhythm. If they wish, they can make buzzing bee sounds, too.

Ant Colony . . . .

Supplies: lab books; pencils and crayons; ant colony (available online and at many toy stores); magnifying glass; books about ants

Setup: Follow the setup directions provided with the ant colony and order live ants. If desired, involve students in the process so that they will be excited about the arrival of the ants. Place the supplies on a table in the center.

Directions: Let students carefully observe the ants at work. Remind them not to touch the colony unless they are helping you feed the ants. Have them use the magnifying glass to closely observe what the ants are doing and encourage them to ask questions. Refer them to the books about ants to learn more. Then, have them draw pictures of what they see in their lab books. If they wish, they can draw the ants as they appear when observed through the magnifying glass.

Hexagon Patterns

Activity found on page 49.

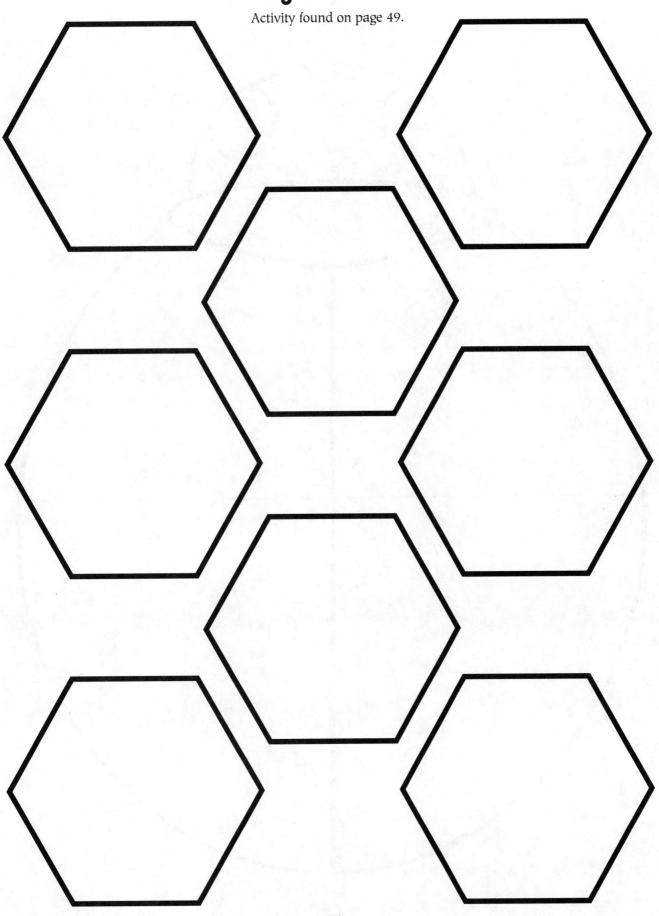

CD-104198 *It's Center Time!*

Ladybug Pattern

Activity found on page 50.

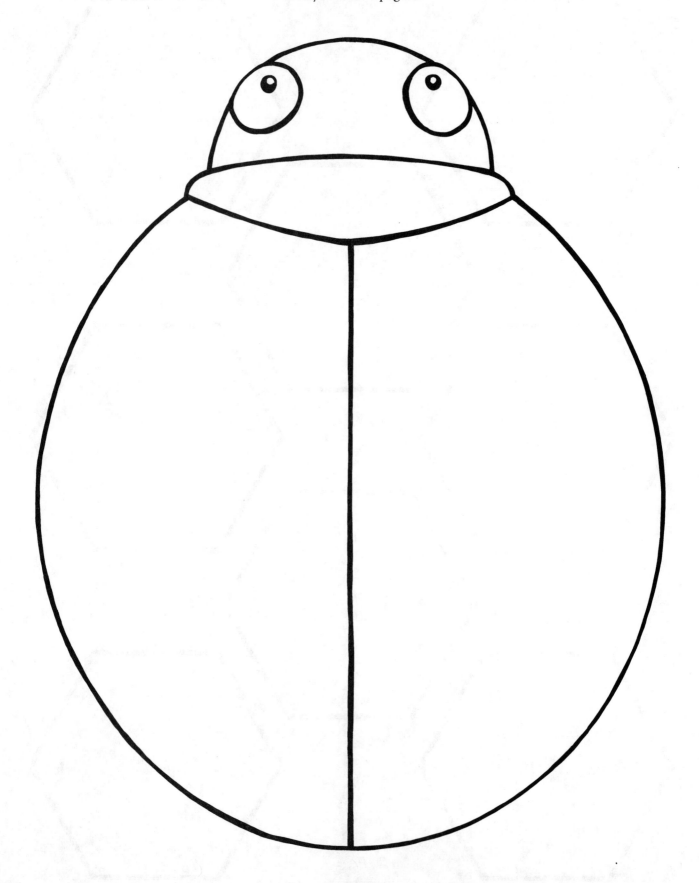

Ocean

🎨 Ocean Mural

Supplies: ocean life mural, markers, crayons, watercolor paints, large paintbrushes, water

Setup: Make large copies of black-and-white ocean life clip art on white copy paper. Glue the copies to white bulletin board paper to make a mural. Lay the mural on a low table or on a protective tarp on the floor. Place the markers and crayons nearby in the center. Reserve the painting supplies for the second part of the activity.

Directions: Instruct students to use the markers and crayons to color the ocean life clip art and add elements of their own, such as plants, coral, and scuba divers. When all of the animals have been colored, provide the painting supplies. Let students cover the entire mural with the watercolor paints. Tell them to observe what happens when they sweep their brushes over the areas colored with crayons versus the areas colored with markers. When the mural is dry, display it on a wall or bulletin board for all to enjoy.

🏠 Boat Construction

Supplies: variety of blocks, small marine life figurines or stuffed animals

Setup: Place all of the supplies in the center.

Directions: Encourage students to use the blocks to build boats. Suggest building a variety of small boats and pushing them around in the "water" area. Or, students can use the blocks to build a large boat that holds all of the builders who are visiting the center. Tell students that they can also use the marine life figurines or stuffed animals as part of the scene.

🎭 The Open Ocean

Supplies: inflatable boat or lightweight canoe; ocean boating supplies, such as plastic oars, life vests, toy fishing poles, plastic or stuffed fish and marine life, nets, buckets, etc.

Setup: Put the boat on the floor in the center. Place the rest of the supplies nearby.

Directions: Encourage students to pretend they are going on a boating excursion in the ocean. Let them create their own scenarios for the trip. What will they see and do while they are out on the open ocean?

👟 🎵 Going Swimming

Supplies: swimming accessories, such as snorkels, masks, goggles, swim fins, life vests, towels, flip-flops, sunglasses, etc.; tape or CD player; tape or CD of beach music

Setup: Place all of the supplies on a table in the center.

Directions: Help students put on the swimming accessories and turn on the music. Encourage them to lie on the floor and "swim" and "float" as though they were in the ocean. Ask them to use their imaginations and describe the fish they see when they look through their masks and goggles.

♥ 123 Octopus Pears . . . .

Supplies: canned pear halves, chocolate chips, plastic knives, plastic foam plates
Setup: Open the canned pears. Place all of the supplies on a table in the center.
Directions: Provide an illustrated recipe card with the following steps on it. Explain the steps to students as you demonstrate the activity. Each student should then follow the recipe.

1. Place a pear half flat side down on a plate.
2. Ask an adult to help you cut 7 slits in the wide part of the pear.
3. Poke the points of 2 chocolate chips into the top of the pear for eyes.
4. Count the octopus's legs before you enjoy your snack!

◇ Library Literature . . . .

Fish Is Fish by Leo Lionni (Dragonfly Books, 1974)
A House for Hermit Crab by Eric Carle (Aladdin, 2005)
The Ocean Alphabet Book by Jerry Pallotta (Charlesbridge Publishing, 1986)
Swimmy by Leo Lionni (Dragonfly Books, 1973)
A Swim through the Sea by Kristin Joy Pratt (Dawn Publications, 1994)

🐚 Exploring Seashells . . . .

Supplies: lab books, pencils and crayons, variety of seashells, magnifying glass
Setup: Place all of the supplies on a table in the center.
Directions: Encourage students to handle and examine all of the different seashells. Remind them to use the magnifying glass to get a closer look. Ask them to consider the differences and similarities among the shells. Let students draw pictures and trace the outlines of the shells in their lab books.

👋 🐚 123 Beach in a Bucket . . . .

Supplies: large bucket of sand and water with an assortment of small plastic manipulatives and figurines
Setup: Fill the bottom third of the bucket with sand. Mix in the manipulatives and figurines. Add water to the bucket until it is about 2/3 full. Place the bucket on a low table or on a towel on the floor in the center.
Directions: Tell students to roll up their sleeves and search for the items buried in the sand. Before they begin, tell them how many items they are searching for. Encourage students to count aloud each time they find a buried item.

Pets

👁 Pet Shop ....

Supplies: stuffed animals and plastic toys of various pets, such as dogs, cats, fish, birds, reptiles, rodents, etc.; pet travel carriers; aquariums or large plastic tubs; empty cages; empty boxes; food and water dishes; pet toys; collars and leashes; grooming supplies, such as brushes, ribbons, and towels; first aid kit

Setup: Create a pet shop by placing the carriers, cages, and aquariums around the perimeter of the center. If these are not available, use empty boxes turned on their sides. Label the carriers with the types of animals that belong in them. Place the toy animals in the appropriate containers. Create a separate area for pet grooming and an area to serve as a veterinarian's office.

Directions: Help students choose roles as employees or patrons of the pet shop. Encourage them to care for the animals, help patrons decide which pets to purchase, answer patrons' questions, and work in the grooming and veterinary areas.

Variation: Instead of using toy animals, have students take turns pretending to be the animals. Encourage them to make sounds and act like the animals in a pet shop.

👟 👁 Act Like the Animals. ....

Supplies: prepared Pet Cards (page 57), bell

Setup: Copy the Pet Cards onto sturdy card stock. Color the cards with markers or crayons and cut them apart. Laminate the cards for durability. Place the cards and the bell on a table in the center.

Directions: Let one student be in charge of the cards and bell. The other students will pretend to be pets. Tell the student with the cards to draw one card from the stack, hold it up, and announce the name of the pictured pet. The other students should begin to act, move, and make sounds like the animal. When the student selects a new card, she should ring the bell to notify the others of the change. Have students trade places after a few turns so that everyone gets a chance to pretend to be pets.

Variation: For a challenge, have the student with the bell switch the cards quickly and see how fast the other students can change roles.

🏠 👁 Caring for Your Pets. ....

Supplies: stuffed animals and plastic toys of various pets, such as dogs, cats, fish, birds, reptiles, rodents, etc.; pet travel carriers; aquariums or large plastic tubs; empty boxes; food and water dishes; pet toys; collars and leashes; grooming supplies, such as brushes, ribbons, and towels

Setup: This center would be ideal next to the pet shop center (above). When a family gets a new pet and brings it home, they must establish responsibilities for the pet. Using the supplies, set up a home scenario complete with the supplies for one or two new pets. (Allow students to select the pets.)

Directions: Encourage students to choose roles as members of a family and work together to establish a routine to care for their new pets. Let students create their own scenarios. If they wish, students can pretend to be the pets instead of using the toy animals.

◇ Library Literature ....

The Best Pet of All by David Larochelle (Dutton Juvenile, 2004)
Millions of Cats by Wanda Gag (Putnam Juvenile, 1996)
The Perfect Pet by Margie Palatini (Katherine Tegen Books, 2003)
Pet Show! by Ezra Jack Keats (Puffin, 2001)
Puppies Are Like That by Jan Pfloog (Random House Books for Young Readers, 1975)

"Pet Treats" for People

Supplies: bowls of cereal flakes (fish), pretzel sticks (dogs), fish-shaped crackers (cats), gummy bugs (reptiles and amphibians), sunflower seeds (rodents), dried apricots, banana chips, and apple chips (birds), coconut and green food coloring (rabbits); spoon for each bowl; resealable plastic bags

Setup: Pour each type of snack into a bowl. Mix the coconut with green food coloring to represent the grass that rabbits eat. Label each bowl with the type of animal and food that it represents. Place all of the supplies on a table in the center.

Directions: Tell students they are going to create bags of "Pet Treats" for themselves! Explain that the foods on the table represent foods that pets eat. But, instead of sharing with their pets, students will get to enjoy these treats. Provide an illustrated recipe card with the following steps on it. Explain the steps to students as you demonstrate the activity. Each student should then follow the recipe.

1. Place 1 spoonful of each type of snack in your bag.
2. Seal the bag and shake it gently to mix the treats.
3. Enjoy your snack!

Pet Graph

Supplies: large bar graph, copies of the Pet Cards (page 57), crayons or markers, glue sticks

Setup: Make several copies of the Pet Cards. Cut apart the cards and sort them by type of animal. Draw a blank bar graph with an x-axis and a y-axis on bulletin board paper. Place the graph on a table in the center or hang it low on a wall or bulletin board where students can reach it. Place the other supplies on a table in the center.

Directions: Have each student select a card for each pet she has at home. (For example, if a student has two dogs and three fish, she should take two dog cards and three fish cards.) Let students color the cards. If a student's pet is not featured on a card, provide a blank index card and help her draw a picture of her pet. Or, if a student does not have any pets, have him select cards for pets that he would like to have. When students are finished coloring, have them glue the cards in rows on the graph to show which type of pet is the most popular in the class.

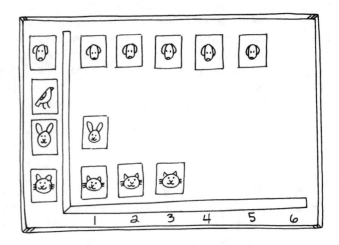

Observing Bird Feeders

Supplies: lab books, pencils and crayons, pinecones, peanut butter, 2 or 3 types of birdseed in foil pie pans, plastic spoons, yarn, masking tape

Setup: Pour the birdseed into the pie pans. Place the supplies on a table in the center.

Directions: Help students make bird feeders. Explain that they will use different kinds of birdseed. Then, they will observe the feeders to determine which kind of seeds birds prefer. If students have pet birds, they can perform this experiment at home and report findings to the class. Or, students can hang the feeders outside a classroom window and "adopt" the neighborhood birds as "class pets." To make the feeders, help students tie yarn around the tops of the pinecones and label each one by writing the type of birdseed on a piece of masking tape. Have students use plastic spoons to coat the pinecones with peanut butter. Then, let students roll each pinecone in the chosen type of birdseed. Hang the feeders outside for the birds and have students observe them daily. Students should record their observations in their lab books by drawing, writing, or dictating about what they see. At the end of one week, ask students to determine which type of birdseed is the favorite among the adopted class pets.

Pet Cards

Activities found on pages 55–56.

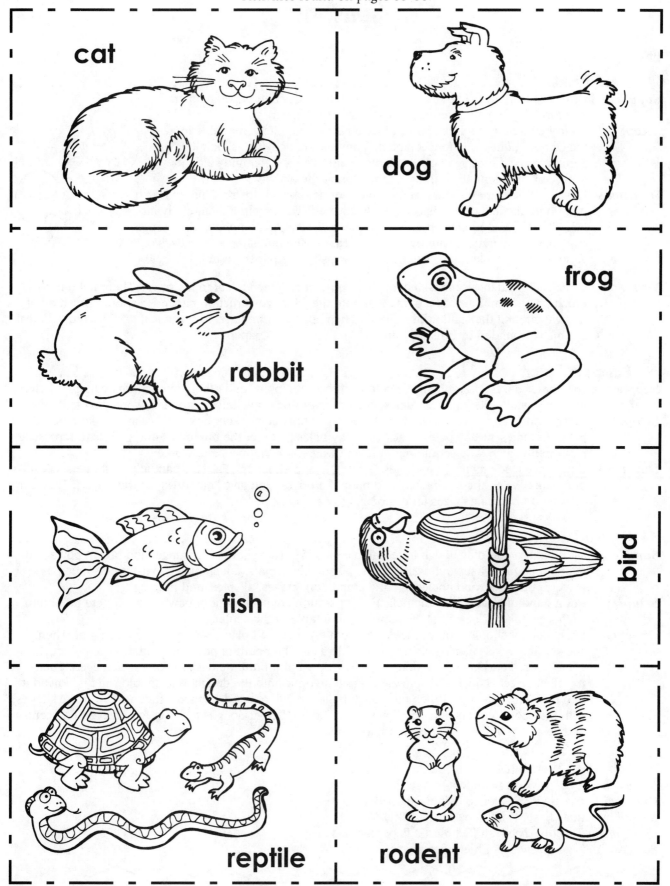

cat

dog

rabbit

frog

fish

bird

reptile

rodent

Seasons

Fall

🎨 Leaf Prints ....

Supplies: variety of fall leaves (real or artificial), white construction paper, tempera paint in foil pie pans, sponge paintbrushes, newspaper

Setup: Pour the paint into foil pie pans. Place all of the supplies on a table in the center. (*Caution:* Before completing any nature activity, ask families' permission and inquire about students' plant allergies. Remind students not to touch potentially harmful plants during the activity.)

Directions: Have each student place a leaf on a piece of newspaper. Instruct him to brush paint onto the leaf until it is completely covered. Then, help him carefully lift the leaf, flip it over, and make a print on a piece of construction paper. Encourage students to experiment with overlapping leaves, different shapes and sizes of leaves, various brush strokes and patterns, etc. Set aside the papers to dry.

Variation: Have each student use masking tape to temporarily attach a leaf to his paper. Then, tell him to brush paint from the middle of the leaf onto the white construction paper. He should brush all of the way around the leaf in this manner. Then, instruct him to remove the leaf and discard it. A leaf outline surrounded by brushed paint will remain on his paper.

🎭 Pumpkin Patch ....

Supplies: "hay bale" boxes; assortment of real or artificial pumpkins and other gourds; money manipulatives; wagon; digital scale; farm costumes, such as overalls, straw hats, bandanas, work gloves, etc.

Setup: Wrap medium-sized cardboard boxes, such as empty copy paper boxes, in yellow bulletin board paper to represent hay bales. Stack the "hay bales," scatter the pumpkins and gourds to represent a pumpkin patch, and set up the scale and wagon for shoppers and workers.

Directions: Encourage students to choose roles as farmers and shoppers. Farmers can help customers select pumpkins, weigh the pumpkins, determine the prices, and give "hay rides" in the wagon. They can also set up hay bale mazes for customers to navigate.

🖐 Fall Dough ....

Supplies: salt dough or molding dough in resealable plastic bags; yellow, red, orange, and brown powdered tempera paint in 4 separate saltshakers; plastic place mats; fall shaped cookie cutters, such as leaves, pumpkins, and apples; ground cinnamon, cloves, allspice, and nutmeg

Setup: Put a handful of dough in each plastic bag. Pour a small amount of powdered tempera paint into each saltshaker. Place all of the supplies on a table in the center.

Directions: Each student should remove the dough from one bag and place it on a plastic place mat. Then, she should choose a saltshaker and sprinkle a small amount of powdered paint onto the dough. Have her roll and knead the dough to mix in the paint until the desired color is achieved. Then, have her select a spice and sprinkle a small amount onto the dough. She should roll and knead it into the dough, as well. When the dough balls are colored and scented, students can make shapes with the cookie cutters, mix small amounts of the different doughs together to achieve new scents and colors, and mold a variety of their own shapes.

◇ Library Literature ....

Animals in the Fall by Gail Saunders-Smith (Capstone Press, 1997)
Fresh Fall Leaves by Betsy Franco (Scholastic, 1994)
It's Fall by Linda Glaser (Millbrook Press, 2001)
It's Pumpkin Time! by Zoe Hall (Scholastic Paperbacks, 1999)
Red Leaf, Yellow Leaf by Lois Ehlert (Scholastic, 1999)

Fall Shakers

Supplies: paper bags (lunch size); twist ties or rubber bands; bowls of assorted fall items from nature, such as hay, acorns, leaves, twigs, etc.; crayons or markers

Setup: Put each type of item from nature into a bowl. Place the supplies on a table in the center.

Directions: Give each student two paper bags to decorate. Next, have him choose two different items from nature and place small amounts of each separately in his two bags. Help him close the bags with the twist ties. Be sure to leave some air in the bags. Then, tell students to shake their bags to hear the differences in the sounds.

Extension: Prepare two bags of each type of item. Close the bags and place them on a table in the center. Encourage students to try to match the bags by listening to the sounds they make when they are shaken.

Pumpkin Patterning

Supplies: bowls of orange construction paper pumpkins, construction paper strips, glue sticks

Setup: Using large sheets of construction paper (any color but orange), cut several long strips of paper that are approximately 3" (7.5 cm) wide. Then, cut out two pumpkins of different sizes from orange construction paper. Use the pumpkins as templates and cut out a large number of both sizes. Put the pumpkins in two bowls. Place the bowls and other supplies on a table in the center.

Directions: Give each student a long strip of paper. Have him select three or four pumpkins and arrange them in a pattern, such as ABAB (big, little, big, little), AABB (big, big, little, little), or ABB (big, little, little). Then, encourage him to duplicate the pattern he created by arranging more pumpkins on the strip of paper. Finally, have each student glue his pumpkins in place.

Leaf Exploration

Supplies: lab books, pencils and crayons, basket or box of various fall leaves (some dried), magnifying glass

Setup: Put the leaves in the basket. Place all of the supplies on a table in the center.

Directions: Tell students to select several different leaves from the basket and examine them with and without the magnifying glass. Encourage students to compare the sizes, shapes, and colors, feel the veins and edges, and smell, manipulate, and crumble the leaves. Have students draw or trace their favorite leaves in their lab books. Ask students if the smells of the leaves remind them of anything. Let them write or dictate their answers in their lab books.

It Feels Like Fall!

Supplies: sensory table; assortment of fall items, such as leaves, acorns, pinecones, sticks, small gourds or pumpkins, pumpkin seeds, etc.

Setup: Place the fall items in the sensory table.

Directions: Encourage students to sort, examine, and manipulate the fall items. Ask them to describe similarities and differences among the items. Remind students to be careful because items like pinecones and sticks may have prickly edges.

Winter

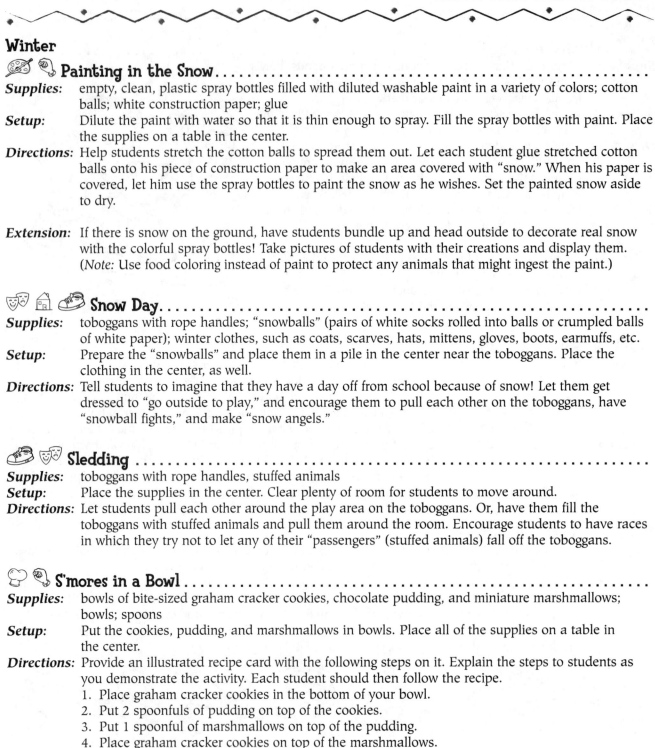 Painting in the Snow...

Supplies: empty, clean, plastic spray bottles filled with diluted washable paint in a variety of colors; cotton balls; white construction paper; glue

Setup: Dilute the paint with water so that it is thin enough to spray. Fill the spray bottles with paint. Place the supplies on a table in the center.

Directions: Help students stretch the cotton balls to spread them out. Let each student glue stretched cotton balls onto his piece of construction paper to make an area covered with "snow." When his paper is covered, let him use the spray bottles to paint the snow as he wishes. Set the painted snow aside to dry.

Extension: If there is snow on the ground, have students bundle up and head outside to decorate real snow with the colorful spray bottles! Take pictures of students with their creations and display them. (*Note:* Use food coloring instead of paint to protect any animals that might ingest the paint.)

Snow Day...

Supplies: toboggans with rope handles; "snowballs" (pairs of white socks rolled into balls or crumpled balls of white paper); winter clothes, such as coats, scarves, hats, mittens, gloves, boots, earmuffs, etc.

Setup: Prepare the "snowballs" and place them in a pile in the center near the toboggans. Place the clothing in the center, as well.

Directions: Tell students to imagine that they have a day off from school because of snow! Let them get dressed to "go outside to play," and encourage them to pull each other on the toboggans, have "snowball fights," and make "snow angels."

Sledding ....

Supplies: toboggans with rope handles, stuffed animals

Setup: Place the supplies in the center. Clear plenty of room for students to move around.

Directions: Let students pull each other around the play area on the toboggans. Or, have them fill the toboggans with stuffed animals and pull them around the room. Encourage students to have races in which they try not to let any of their "passengers" (stuffed animals) fall off the toboggans.

S'mores in a Bowl...

Supplies: bowls of bite-sized graham cracker cookies, chocolate pudding, and miniature marshmallows; bowls; spoons

Setup: Put the cookies, pudding, and marshmallows in bowls. Place all of the supplies on a table in the center.

Directions: Provide an illustrated recipe card with the following steps on it. Explain the steps to students as you demonstrate the activity. Each student should then follow the recipe.
1. Place graham cracker cookies in the bottom of your bowl.
2. Put 2 spoonfuls of pudding on top of the cookies.
3. Put 1 spoonful of marshmallows on top of the pudding.
4. Place graham cracker cookies on top of the marshmallows.
5. Use a spoon to enjoy your snack!

Library Literature ....

The First Day of Winter by Denise Fleming (Henry Holt and Co., 2005)

The Mitten by Jan Brett (Scholastic, 1990)

Snow by Roy McKie and P. D. Eastman (Random House Books for Young Readers, 1962)

The Snowy Day by Ezra Jack Keats (Puffin, 1976)

Thomas' Snowsuit by Robert Munsch (Annick Press, 1985)

123 🎨 Sequencing Snowmen . . . .

Supplies: blue construction paper; crayons; foil pie pans or bowls of cotton balls, black paper hats, and small twigs; glue; scissors

Setup: Create four rectangles for each student by folding a piece of blue construction paper in half twice. Cut out small snowman hats from black construction paper, each approximately 1½" x 1½" (3.75 cm x 3.75 cm). Break the twigs into 2" (5 cm) pieces. Place the hats, twigs, and cotton balls in pans or bowls. Place all of the supplies on a table in the center. (*Caution:* Before completing any nature activity, ask families' permission and inquire about students' plant allergies. Remind students not to touch potentially harmful plants during the activity.)

Directions: Explain to students that they are going to show the steps of how to make a snowman. First, help them number the four sections of their papers with crayons. Then, help students cut apart the four rectangles on the fold lines and place them number side down on the table. On rectangle 1, have each student glue one cotton ball to represent the base of a snowman. On rectangle 2, students should glue two cotton balls. On rectangle 3, students should glue three cotton balls. Finally, on rectangle 4, students should glue three cotton balls, a hat, and two twig arms. Then, when the glue is dry, let each student use the four rectangles as a puzzle to sequence. They can self-check the sequence by turning over the rectangles to see if the numbers are in order.

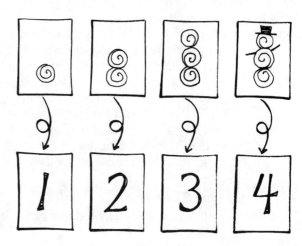

🍃 ✋ ✏️ Melting Ice . . . .

Supplies: lab books, pencils and crayons, tinted ice cubes, 2 small baking trays, sandpaper, aluminum foil, thick rubber gloves or waterproof gloves, clear plastic bowl or cup, paper towels

Setup: Use food coloring to make colorful water. Pour the colorful water into ice cube trays and freeze until solid. Place sandpaper in the bottom of one baking tray and foil in the bottom of the other baking tray. Fill the bowl or cup half full of water. Lay a paper towel on the table. Place all of the supplies on a table in the center.

Directions: Tell students that they will experiment to find what melts ice the fastest—water, air, or friction. After you explain the experiment and before students actually begin the tests, have students guess which method will be the fastest and which will be the slowest. Let them record their guesses in their lab books. Help students place one ice cube on the paper towel, one in the bowl of water, one on the sandpaper, and one on the foil. Have two students put on gloves and rub the ice cubes over the sandpaper and foil. At least one other student should observe all four cubes during the experiment to see which melts the fastest and which melts the slowest. Encourage students to write, dictate, or draw in their lab books about what happened during the experiment.

✏️ ✊ ✋ Snow Writing . . . .

Supplies: white shaving foam (not gel), baking trays, cotton swabs

Setup: Spray shaving foam on the trays. Place all of the supplies on a table in the center.

Directions: Have students use their hands to spread the shaving foam "snow" on the trays. Then, let them use their fingers or cotton swabs to write letters, numbers, and words in the snow. Encourage them to write the alphabet, their names, and other familiar words. When a tray is full of writing, students can "erase" by smoothing their hands over the snow to spread it flat. Remind students not to touch their faces or eyes during this activity.

Spring

Spring Abstracts ....

Supplies: muslin squares, colorful fresh flowers and leaves, piece of wood (like a cutting board), newspaper, rolling pin, heavy card stock or frame matting, glue

Setup: Cut muslin into 12" (30 cm) square pieces. Cut card stock into 13" (33 cm) squares. If desired, cut out the middles of the card stock squares to create frames with edges that are 2" (5 cm) wide. Spread newspaper on the table and floor in the center. Place the other supplies on a table in the center. (*Caution:* Before completing any nature activity, ask families' permission and inquire about students' plant allergies. Remind students not to touch potentially harmful plants during the activity.)

Directions: Give each student a piece of muslin. Have her select several flowers and leaves and place them on the muslin. Tell her to fold the fabric in half, sandwiching the flowers and leaves inside. Then, have her place the folded muslin on top of the newspaper on the floor. Let her place the piece of wood over the fabric and stomp on it several times to crush the flowers and leaves. When she removes the wood, the colorful pigments from the flowers and leaves will be transferred onto the fabric, leaving abstract shapes and colors. Students can also place the fabric on top of the newspaper on the table and roll over it with the rolling pin to release the pigments. Let students repeat this process with new flowers and leaves until they are satisfied with the colors and designs they have created. Help each student stretch the muslin on top of a large square of card stock or across the back of a card stock frame and glue it in place. Set the creations aside to allow the glue and pigments to dry.

Spring Cloisonné ....

Supplies: yarn, white construction paper, bowl of liquid fabric starch, colorful tissue paper squares in foil pie pans, paintbrushes

Setup: Cut the yarn into 20" (50 cm) pieces. Pour the starch into a bowl. Cut the tissue paper into 1"–2" (2.5 cm–5 cm) squares. Distribute the tissue paper squares into several pie pans. Place all of the supplies on a table in the center.

Directions: Explain to students that cloisonné is a form of art in which areas of raised wire are filled with different colors. Tell students that they will make their own cloisonné masterpieces using yarn and tissue paper. Instruct each student to submerge a piece of yarn in liquid starch. Then, he should squeeze out the excess starch and lay the yarn on his paper in a design. Remind students that the yarn should crisscross over itself several times to make different shapes on the paper. Tell students to press down on the yarn to be sure it sticks to the paper well. Then, each student should use a paintbrush to paint starch into one of the spaces on his paper. Have him place tissue paper over the starch, filling in the opening created by the string. Explain that it is OK for the tissue paper to wrinkle, and it is OK to use more than one piece of tissue paper to fill a space. When the space is filled, tell the student to use the paintbrush to paint starch over the top of the tissue paper. Let students continue this process until all of the spaces on their papers are filled with tissue paper. Set aside the cloisonné masterpieces to dry.

Library Literature ....

Hopper Hunts for Spring by Marcus Pfister (North-South Books, 1995)
It's Spring! by Linda Glaser (Millbrook Press, 2002)
My Spring Robin by Anne Rockwell (Aladdin, 1996)
Spring Is Here by Taro Gomi (Chronicle Books, 1995)
When Will It Be Spring? by Catherine Walters (Scholastic, 1999)

Mud Cups

Supplies: bowls of chocolate pudding, chocolate wafer cookie crumbs, and gummy worms; paper cups; spoons

Setup: Crush chocolate wafer cookies to make crumbs. Put the pudding, cookie crumbs, and gummy worms in separate bowls. Place all of the supplies on a table in the center.

Directions: Provide an illustrated recipe card with the following steps on it. Explain the steps to students as you demonstrate the activity. Each student should then follow the recipe.
1. Put 2 spoonfuls of pudding in your cup.
2. Put 1 spoonful of cookie crumbs in your cup.
3. Stir the pudding and cookie crumbs together.
4. Add gummy worms to your cup and use a spoon to enjoy your snack!

Counting Flowers

Supplies: 10 plastic vases, labeled from 1 to 10; large box or basket of assorted artificial flowers (available at most craft stores)

Setup: Use index cards to label the vases from 1 to 10. Put the flowers in the box or basket. Place the flowers and vases on a table in the center.

Directions: Have students count aloud as they put the appropriate number of flowers in each vase. After all of the vases are full, have students remove the flowers, rearrange the vases, and start over.

Extension: Label the vases with simple number sentences, such as *1 + 1*. Have students solve the number sentences and place the correct number of flowers in the vases.

Flower Dance

Supplies: tape or CD player; tape or CD of spring music, such as "Spring" from *The Four Seasons* by Antonio Vivaldi; flower leis; assortment of artificial flowers

Setup: Place all of the supplies on a table in the center.

Directions: Help students adorn themselves with flower leis by twisting them around their arms, legs, and heads, and wearing them around their necks. Explain that you will start the music and they should dance and play as they feel inspired. They can scatter the artificial flowers around the room, toss them gently in the air, or exchange them with classmates as they dance.

Raindrops

Supplies: lab books, pencils and crayons, large plastic bowl or container of water, sensory table with sand and potting soil or dirt, eyedroppers, basting tools

Setup: Fill the bowl half full of water and put it in the middle of the sensory table. Fill one side of the sensory table with sand and the other side with potting soil or dirt. Pack the sand and dirt around the bowl of water. Place the other supplies on a table near the sensory table in the center.

Directions: Explain that students will be observing what happens when raindrops land in different places, such as on the beach (sand), on the ground (dirt), or on the ocean (water). They will also examine the difference between small and large raindrops. Tell students to use the eyedroppers to make small raindrops. Let them squirt small droplets over the sand, dirt, and water and observe what happens. Encourage students to draw, write, and dictate about their findings in their lab books. Then, let them use the basting tools to make larger raindrops that fall with more force, like a hard rainstorm. What differences and similarities do they observe? Have students record their findings in their lab books.

Summer

 Sunshine Fade Art . . . .

Supplies: construction paper shapes, construction paper, tape

Setup: Cut out a variety of shapes from construction paper. Place the supplies on a table in the center.

Directions: Each student should use small pieces of tape to attach a variety of precut shapes to a piece of construction paper. When the pieces are complete, have students tape their artwork to a window that gets plenty of direct sunlight. The artwork should be facing toward the outside. After one week, let students remove the art from the windows. Each student should carefully remove the shapes from her artwork to observe the changes. Ask students why they think the construction paper looks different. What do they think caused the changes?

 At the Beach . . . .

Supplies: blue blankets, tarp, towels, or bulletin board paper (water); tan blankets, towels, or bulletin board paper (sand); seashells; beach toys; beach towels; umbrellas; child-sized beach chairs; picnic basket; toy food and drinks; inflatable rafts, beach balls, and rings; beach bags; empty, clean sunscreen bottles; sunglasses; large-brimmed hats; blocks

Setup: Create a beach scene by spreading the blue and tan blankets to represent the ocean and sand. Scatter seashells on the "sand." Place the toys and other accessories in the center, as well.

Directions: Encourage students to "spend a day at the beach" by setting up their chairs, umbrellas, and towels. Let them enjoy a picnic lunch, lounge in the sun, build sand castles with the blocks and beach toys, and play in the "ocean." Remind them to wear their sunscreen!

 **Lemonade** . . . .

Supplies: powdered lemonade; bowls of lemons, water, and ice; paper or plastic cups; spoons; 1/2-cup measuring cup

Setup: Slice the lemons into wedges. Put the lemon wedges, water, and ice in separate bowls. Place all of the supplies on a table in the center.

Directions: Provide an illustrated recipe card with the following steps on it. Explain the steps to students as you demonstrate the activity. Each student should then follow the recipe.
1. Spoon 1 spoonful of powdered lemonade into your cup.
2. Use the measuring cup to scoop ½ cup of water into your cup.
3. Stir your lemonade.
4. Add ice and a lemon wedge and enjoy your drink!

123 Ice Cream Math . . . .

Supplies: construction paper ice cream cones and scoops, felt board

Setup: Cut out ice cream cone shapes from colorful construction paper. Then, cut out circles to represent scoops of ice cream. On each cone, write a number from 1 to 10. Laminate the cones and scoops for durability. Attach the hook side of hook-and-loop tape to the back of each cone and scoop so that the pieces will stick to felt. Place the cones, scoops, and felt board on a table in the center.

Directions: Help students spread the cones facedown on the table. Have one student select a cone. Tell him to flip it over, read the number on it, and attach it to the felt board. Then, he should count the corresponding number of scoops of ice cream and add them to the cone. Let each student continue playing until all of the cones have been used.

◇ **Library Literature** . . . .
Come On, Rain! by Karen Hesse (Scholastic, 1999)
How Do You Know It's Summer? by Allan Fowler (Children's Press, 1992)
One Hot Summer Day by Nina Crews (Greenwillow, 1995)
Summer by Alice Low (Random House Books for Young Readers, 2001)
Summer Stinks by Marty Kelley (Zino Press Children's Books, 2001)

♪ 👟 **Beach Ball Bounce** . . . .
Supplies: small inflatable beach balls, tennis rackets, tape or CD player, tape or CD of popular beach music
Setup: Inflate the beach balls. Place the supplies in the center. Clear plenty of room for this activity.
Directions: Let students practice bouncing the beach balls on the rackets. Then, turn on the music and let them bounce the beach balls to the beat of the music. Depending on students' abilities, allow them to dribble the beach balls instead of using the rackets. Encourage students to dance to the music whenever they need a break from bouncing the beach balls.

🍃 **Attracting the Sun** . . . .
Supplies: lab books; pencils and crayons; envelopes of colorful construction paper strips (must use black, white, and 3 other colors); resealable plastic bags of chocolate chips; warm, sunny place outside or gooseneck lamps with high-wattage bulbs
Setup: Cut the construction paper into strips, each approximately 2" x 3" (5 cm x 7.5 cm). Place one strip of each color in an envelope. Prepare an envelope for each student. Place 5 chocolate chips in a resealable plastic bag for each student. If using lamps, place them on a table in the center, plug them in, and turn them on so that they can heat up. (*Caution:* Never leave students unattended around a hot lamp. Touching a hot lightbulb can cause burns.) Place the rest of the supplies on a table in the center.
Directions: Students can conduct this experiment outside if it is a hot, sunny day, or they can do it under warm lamps inside. Each student should remove her strips of paper from the envelope and align them in a row on the ground in the sun or on the table under the lamps. She should then place one chocolate chip on top of each strip of paper. If using lamps, bend the necks of the lamps so that the bulbs are close to the surface of the table without touching it. While waiting for the results, have each student draw a small circle of each color in her lab book to match each of the strips in the experiment. Tell students to observe the chocolate chips to see which one begins to melt first. Which color paper caused the chocolate chip to melt first? Which started to melt last? Have each student draw a circle around the color that caused melting to start first and an *X* over the color that caused melting to start last. Let students discuss their findings.

✏ 👒 **Muddy Words** . . . .
Supplies: plastic or plastic foam plates, bowl of chocolate pudding, spoon, rubber spatulas or plastic knives
Setup: Put the chocolate pudding in a bowl. Place all of the supplies on a table in the center.
Directions: Let each student spoon 2 to 3 spoonfuls of pudding onto a plate. Have her use a spatula or plastic knife to smooth the pudding across the plate. Then, encourage each student to use a finger to write letters, numbers, and familiar words in the pudding. Students can also practice drawing shapes and doodling to increase letter-writing skills. Let each student use a spatula or plastic knife to smooth the pudding when the plate is covered with writing and drawings so that she can continue the activity.

Shapes

Stained Glass Pictures.

Supplies: colorful crepe paper streamer shapes in foil pie pans, bowls of water, eyedroppers, white construction paper

Setup: Cut out a variety of familiar shapes from crepe paper streamers. Use several colors for each different shape. Depending on students' abilities, you may want to have them help you cut out these shapes. Sort the shapes and place them in pie pans. Fill a few bowls half full of warm water. Place all of the supplies on a table in the center.

Directions: Let each student select a shape. Tell her to place it on a piece of white paper and use an eyedropper to carefully drop a few drops of water onto the shape. Each shape will need just enough water to make the colors start to bleed. Have each student continue this process until she has a variety of shapes and colors covering the paper. When students are finished, have them carefully remove the crepe-paper shapes from their papers. Beautiful "stained glass" designs will remain on their papers!

Pasta Sorting

Supplies: bowl of at least 2 types of uncooked shaped pasta, such as wagon wheels (ruote), disks (orecchiette), short tubes (mezzi rigatoni), honeycombs (fiori), or bow ties (farfalle); 2 empty bowls; shelf that will fit over the 3 bowls; large towel or blanket

Setup: Mix two types of pasta in one bowl. Place the bowl of pasta and two empty bowls under the shelf on a table in the center. Cover the shelf with the towel or blanket so that students cannot see what is underneath it.

Directions: Explain to students that they will sort a bowl of pasta based on the shapes they feel, but they cannot look at the pasta while sorting it. They have to rely on their fingers to help them. Show them the two types of pasta and let them handle a piece of each so that they know how the shape of each one feels. Then, let one student place his hands under the towel and sort the pasta from the first bowl into the two empty bowls. When he is finished, let him remove the towel to see how he did. For a challenge, have students sort more than two types of pasta at one time.

Ham and Cheese Wheels.

Supplies: small flour tortillas, cream cheese spread, deli-sliced ham (or other meat), individual cheese slices, plastic knives, paper or plastic foam plates

Setup: Place the supplies on a table in the center.

Directions: Provide an illustrated recipe card with the following steps on it. Explain the steps to students as you demonstrate the activity. Each student should then follow the recipe.
1. Place 1 tortilla on your plate and spread cream cheese on it.
2. Add 2 slices of ham and 1 slice of cheese in the middle of the tortilla.
3. Roll up the tortilla.
4. Ask an adult to help you slice your tortilla into wheels.
5. Enjoy your snack!

Note: If the tortillas are unrolling, wrap them tightly in plastic wrap after Step 3 and refrigerate for a few hours to set the cream cheese. Then, remove the plastic wrap and proceed with Step 4. Or, use toothpicks to hold the wheels together. Be sure to remove the toothpicks before students eat their snacks.

◇ Library Literature . . . .
The Shape of Things by Dayle Ann Dodds (Scholastic, 1994)
Shapes by Chuck Murphy (Little Simon, 2001)
Shapes, Shapes, Shapes by Tana Hoban (HarperTrophy, 1996)
So Many Circles, So Many Squares by Tana Hoban (Greenwillow, 1998)
Squarehead by Harriet Ziefert (Houghton Mifflin/Walter Lorraine Books, 2001)

♪ 👟 Shape Twister . . . .
Supplies: colorful poster board shapes taped to the floor, premade tape, tape player
Setup: Prepare a tape by recording yourself giving instructions for each shape, such as, "Put one hand on the circle," "Tiptoe to the triangle," or "Put both feet on the square." Repeat each direction at least once. Leave a long pause between each direction. You may also choose to play music in the background while you record the tape. Cut out approximately 12" x 12" (30 cm x 30 cm) shapes from poster board. Include familiar shapes and figures, such as a circle, square, rectangle, triangle, oval, heart, and star. Laminate the shapes for durability. Scatter the shapes on the floor in a large play area and tape them securely in place. Place the other supplies on a table in the center.
Directions: Help students start the tape and begin following the directions. If there are more than three players at a time, consider having students take turns following the instructions on the tape to avoid chaos.

♪ Shaped Music . . . .
Supplies: tambourines, triangles, square wood blocks, xylophones, colorful construction paper shapes, enlarged copy of the Musical Staff Pattern (page 16)
Setup: Cut several 1" (2.5 cm) circles, squares, triangles, and rectangles from construction paper. If desired, color code the shapes for easier recognition. Laminate the shapes and Musical Staff Pattern for durability. Attach hook-and-loop tape to the backs of the shapes and to the front of the Musical Staff Pattern. Hang the Musical Staff Pattern on a wall in the center. Place the shapes and the instruments on a table in the center.
Directions: Explain that each musical instrument is similar to a familiar shape—tambourine (circle), triangle (triangle), wood blocks (square), and xylophone tiles (rectangle). Tell students that the colorful shapes represent musical notes and each shape corresponds to an instrument. Play a few notes to demonstrate. Have students attach the shapes to the lines and spaces on the musical staff in any order they wish. Then, tell students to play the song by following the notes in the sequence, matching the shapes of the notes to the shapes of the instruments.

✋ Crater Shapes . . . .
Supplies: sensory table, sand, water, shaped cookie cutters, plastic spoons
Setup: Pour sand into the sensory table and add water to wet the sand. Pat it smooth. Place the cookie cutters and spoons on top of the sand.
Directions: Tell students to press the cookie cutter shapes into the wet sand. Then, let them use the spoons to carefully scoop out the sand in the middle of each cookie cutter to reveal a shaped hole. Have students identify each shape aloud as they make it. When the sand is full of holes, they can pat it smooth and start again.

Space

Earth, Moon, & Sun Model...

Supplies: copies of the Space Model Pattern (page 70) on white card stock; markers or crayons; scissors; hole punch; paper fasteners

Setup: Copy one Space Model Pattern onto white card stock for each student. Place the supplies on a table in the center.

Directions: Talk to students about how the moon orbits, or circles around, Earth, and Earth orbits the sun. Explain that each student will make a model to show these orbits. First, each student should color the pieces of her model. Then, she should carefully cut out the pieces and punch four holes where indicated on the two tab pieces. (Students may require adult help when using a hole punch.) Next, help each student push a paper fastener through the dot on the moon and attach the small tab to the back. She should then push a second paper fastener through the dot on Earth, attach it to the other end of the small tab, and then attach one end of the large tab. Finally, each student should push a third paper fastener through the dot on the sun and attach it to the other end of the large tab. Tell students to move the moon to orbit Earth and Earth to orbit the sun.

Spaceship ....

Supplies: "spaceship," "space helmets," disposable paint coveralls (optional; available at most home improvement stores)

Setup: Create a "spaceship," space scene, and costumes for students. Cut a small porthole window in the side of an empty appliance box. Paint the inside and outside of the box as desired. Remember to paint a variety of instrument panels with gears and gauges inside the box. Arrange glow sticks (available at most party supply stores) or small flashlights inside and outside the box and secure them in place with tape. Be sure to use enough lights inside the spaceship for students to be able to see when the door is closed behind them. Place an old computer keyboard or a box the same size and shape as a keyboard inside the spaceship for the "astronauts" to use as a control panel. Attach one end of a jump rope to the door of the spaceship to tether the astronauts when they go on "space walks." Cut out a variety of stars, planets, and moons from poster board and tape them to the floor outside the spaceship to create a space scene. Finally, create "space helmets" by cutting viewing holes in the sides of large paper grocery bags. Trim the bags to a height of approximately 12"–14" (30 cm–35 cm). Decorate the helmets as desired. Or, have each student create her own helmet as an activity in the art center. Place the supplies in the center.

Directions: Have students put on the "space suits" and helmets. Let them decide where they will travel and what they will see on their journey. Encourage them to "explore space" by taking space walks (attached to the tether so that they won't float away) and to "visit other places in the galaxy."

🍳 Star Sandwiches..

Supplies: sliced bread; individual cheese slices or spreads, such as peanut butter, jelly, or cream cheese; star-shaped cookie cutters; paper or plastic foam plates; plastic knives (if using spreads)

Setup: Place the supplies on a table in the center.

Directions: Provide an illustrated recipe card with the following steps on it. Explain the steps to students as you demonstrate the activity. Each student should then follow the recipe.

1. Place 1 slice of cheese on top of 1 slice of bread. (Or, spread a topping on the bread.)
2. Place a second slice of bread on top of the cheese (or spread).
3. Use a cookie cutter to make a star-shaped sandwich.
4. Enjoy your space snack!

◇ Library Literature..

Goodnight Moon by Margaret Wise Brown (HarperTrophy, 2006)
No Moon, No Milk! by Chris Babcock (Dragonfly Books, 1995)
The Space Shuttle by Allison Lassieur (Children's Press, 2001)
There's No Place Like Space: All About Our Solar System by Tish Rabe
    (Random House Books for Young Readers, 1999)
Twinkle, Twinkle, Little Star by Iza Trapani (Charlesbridge Publishing, 1997)

123 👟 Map the Stars..

Supplies: numbered star path

Setup: Cut out 20 large stars from card stock or poster board. Number the stars from 1 to 20 and laminate them for durability. Spread the stars on the floor randomly throughout the center and tape them securely in place.

Directions: Instruct each student to start by finding the star labeled number 1. Then, have him move from star to star, in order, until he reaches star number 20. Encourage students to move in different ways, like an astronaut on the moon or like a shooting star. For a challenge, have students work backward finding stars from number 20 to number 1.

🎵 🎨 👟 Flying Saucer Shakers..

Supplies: paper plates; markers or crayons; star stamps and ink pads (optional); dried beans; crepe paper streamers; stapler; tape or CD player; tape or CD of space music, such as the theme song from *2001: A Space Odyssey (Original Motion Picture Sound Track)* (Rhino Records, 1996)

Setup: Place the supplies on a table in the center.

Directions: Have each student decorate the bottoms of two paper plates. Next, each student should cut five pieces of crepe paper streamer, each approximately 24" (60 cm) long. Help students staple the streamers to the outer edges of their bottom plates. Then, help each student spread dried beans in the bottom plate. Finally, staple the second plate on top, being careful to seal the edges tightly so that the beans do not fall out.
When the flying saucer shakers are complete, help students turn on the space music and encourage them to move their shakers around and dance to the rhythm of the music. Invite students to imagine themselves visiting other planets, moons, and stars, racing spaceships, and discovering new galaxies.

69

Space Model Pattern

Activity found on page 68.

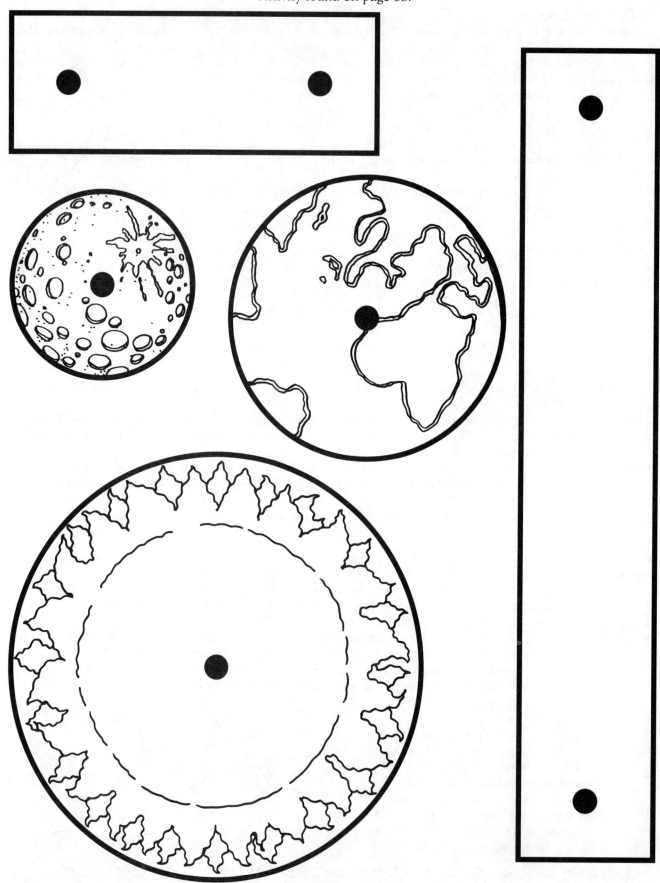

Transportation

🎨 Tire Painting . . . .

Supplies: variety of toy vehicles that have wheels (look for tires that have different kinds of treads), tempera paints in large foil roasting pans, paper, large bowl of water, towels

Setup: Pour a thin layer of paint in the bottom of each roasting pan. Fill a bowl half full of water. Place the supplies on a table in the center.

Directions: Let each student choose a toy vehicle and roll it gently in a tray of paint to coat the wheels. Then, tell him to "drive" the toy over his paper in any direction he chooses. (Remind students not to press too hard so that the tires will leave patterns on their papers.) Students can recoat the tires with the same color paint or dip the toy in the bowl of water to rinse off the residue. After he has dried the toy with a towel, he can select a different toy and a different of color paint or use the same toy with a different color of paint. When students are finished, set aside the paintings to dry.

🎭 Car Repair Shop . . . .

Supplies: small ride-on toys, such as cars, tricycles, bicycles with training wheels, wagons, etc.; toy tools; jumpsuits or overalls; toy cash register and money manipulatives; empty, clean plastic bottles; short garden hoses; buckets; rags; towels; sponges; handheld vacuum; skateboard or wheeled sled; paper; crayons or markers; chairs; magazines

Setup: Create a car repair shop and car wash area for the ride-on toys. Set up a garage area with tools, plastic bottles (for "oil" and other "fluids"), hoses (for "air" and "water"), and a skateboard or wheeled sled for mechanics to lie on while working on the lower parts of the vehicles. Establish a car wash area with hoses, buckets, rags, towels, sponges, and a handheld vacuum. Place the cash register and money manipulatives on a table to represent the checkout area. Nearby, set up the chairs and magazines in a customer waiting area. Also, place the paper and crayons or markers in this area so that customers can create their own personalized license plates while they wait. (Visit official state and province Web sites to find sample images of license plates to print and display for students.)

Directions: Help students decide who will play each role. They will need at least one mechanic, a cashier, several car wash technicians, and customers. Mechanics will need jumpsuits or overalls to protect their clothing. Encourage the customers to bring in their vehicles for service and then describe and demonstrate the funny sounds and other problems that they need to have fixed. Have the mechanics work on the vehicles and let the cashiers assist the customers in designing personalized license plates.

🍽️ Celery Boats . . . .

Supplies: paper plates or towels, plastic knives or spoons, celery, peanut butter or cream cheese spread, raisins or small grapes

Setup: Wash and cut the celery into 2"–3" (5 cm–7.5 cm) pieces. Place the supplies on a table in the center.

Directions: Provide an illustrated recipe card with the following steps on it. Explain the steps to students as you demonstrate the activity. Each student should then follow the recipe.
1. Use a knife or spoon to scoop some peanut butter or cream cheese.
2. Spread the peanut butter or cream cheese in the groove of the celery.
3. Place raisins or grapes on top of the peanut butter or cream cheese. These are the "passengers" in the "celery boat."
4. Enjoy your snack!

◇ Library Literature ....

3, 2, 1 Go!: A Transportation Countdown by Sarah L. Schuette (Capstone Press, 2003)
The Big Book of Things That Go compiled by DK Publishing (DK Children, 1994)
The Little Airplane by Lois Lenski (Random House Books for Young Readers, 2003)
The Little Engine That Could by Watty Piper (Philomel, 2005)
The Wheels on the Bus by Paul O. Zelinsky (Dutton Juvenile, 1990)

1 Honk, 2 Honks, 3 Honks ....

Supplies: premade tape, tape player
Setup: Prepare a tape by recording the sound of a car honking once, twice, or three times in a row. Leave approximately 10 seconds between each series of honks. Use masking tape to create 3 large squares on the floor of the center. Inside each square, tape a number 1, 2, or 3. Place the tape player and premade tape on a table in the center.
Directions: Instruct students to start the tape and listen for the car honks. Tell them to count the number of honks they hear and then go to the corresponding square. Encourage them to move from square to square as if they are operating a variety of vehicles, such as a fast car, a huge truck, a boat, or an airplane.

123 Navigating the Numbers ....

Supplies: variety of toy vehicles
Setup: Write numbers from 1 to 10 on pieces of paper. Scatter the pieces of paper randomly around the center on the floor and tape them securely in place. Make "roads" between the numbers by stretching pieces of masking tape from number to number in order.
Directions: Have each student choose a toy vehicle and find the number 1 on the floor. Tell students to travel along the number roads by driving, flying, or steering their vehicles from 1 to 10. Encourage them to make noises like their vehicles and count aloud as they reach each number. For a challenge, have students travel backward from 10 to 1.

Speedy Slopes ....

Supplies: lab books, pencils and crayons, variety of toy vehicles that have wheels, large blocks, wood planks or baking sheets
Setup: Place the supplies in the center.
Directions: Demonstrate how to make a slope by propping one end of a plank or baking sheet on a short stack of blocks. Ask students what they think will happen if you place a toy vehicle at the top of the slope. Let them draw their predictions in their lab books before you demonstrate. After the demonstration, let students build their own slopes and experiment with the different types of vehicles and different slope lengths and heights. What will be different if they release a toy vehicle on a steep slope and then release the same vehicle on a shallow slope? Encourage them to make predictions in their lab books before each experiment and discuss why they think each result occurred.

Weather

🎨 Wind Art ....

Supplies: shallow box or bin that is at least 9" x 12" (23 cm x 30 cm), paper, bowls of thinned tempera paint, plastic spoons, plastic drinking straws

Setup: Pour the thinned paints into bowls. Place the supplies on a table in the center.

Directions: Have a student put one piece of paper in the bottom of the box. (The edges of the box will keep the paints from splattering.) Tell her to use a spoon to place a small amount of paint on the paper. Then, let her use a straw to blow the paint to spread it across the paper. Encourage students to experiment by blowing directly over the paint, from side to side, quickly, softly, etc. When a student completes her wind art, remove it from the box and set it aside to dry.

🎨 123 ✏️ How Many Snowflakes in a Snowstorm? ....

Supplies: black or dark blue construction paper, white chalk

Setup: Place the supplies on a table in the center.

Directions: Show students how to draw a snowflake. Remind them that no two snowflakes are alike, so they can draw snowflakes in a variety of ways. Have each student use chalk to draw a snowstorm on his paper. Then, tell him to number the snowflakes on his paper. (*Tip:* Spray aerosol hair spray on students' papers to keep chalk from smearing.) Encourage students to count aloud the number of snowflakes in their snowstorms.

🎭 Weather Station ....

Supplies: outdoor thermometer; weather pages from a newspaper; local, state, and national maps; copies of the Weather Cards (page 75); suit jackets and ties (for boys); suit jackets and scarves (for girls); video camera and TV (optional)

Setup: Make several copies of the Weather Cards. Color and cut apart the cards. Laminate the cards and the maps for durability. Place hook-and-loop tape on the backs of the Weather Cards and on well-known locations on the maps (your own location, capitals, big cities, national capital, etc.). Hang the maps on a wall in the center. Hang the thermometer outside a classroom window so that students can read it each day. If you are using a video camera and TV, set them up so that the camera shows real-time footage on the TV screen. (Your camera's instruction manual will provide directions.) Point the camera at the maps so that students can "broadcast" the weather "live" on TV. Place the other supplies in the center.

Directions: Encourage students to prepare the weather report by checking the thermometer and observing the weather outside. Help them review the weather pages in the newspaper to learn about the weather around the country. Show them how to attach the Weather Cards to the maps to indicate where it is sunny, rainy, cloudy, and snowy. When the weather report is ready, encourage students to get ready for the broadcast by putting on jackets and ties or scarves. Let them stand in front of the camera and give a live weather report. (If you are not using a camera and TV, students can still pretend to give the live report.)

✊ ✋ Rainbow Droplets ....

Supplies: 5 clear plastic cups of colorful water, 1 clear plastic cup of clean water, six eyedroppers

Setup: Fill six cups half full of water. Add green, blue, purple, red, orange, and yellow food coloring to the cups. Add enough food coloring to make bright colors. Fill another cup half full of water and do not add any food coloring. Put an eyedropper with each cup of colorful water. Place all of the supplies on a table in the center.

Directions: Have students use the eyedroppers to drop colorful "raindrops" into the cup of clean water. Tell them to drop the droplets one by one and watch them swirl and mix into the clear water. Encourage them to mix the colors and watch what happens as various colors are added. Rinse the cup and refill with clean water for each student.

🍳 Rainbow Salad . . . .

Supplies: bowls of strawberries, mandarin orange slices, pineapple chunks, kiwi fruit slices, blueberries, and purple seedless grapes; plastic spoons; paper plates

Setup: Clean and slice the fruit as needed. Put each type of fruit in a separate bowl with a spoon. Place the supplies on a table in the center.

Directions: Tell students that they are going to make rainbows with fruit. Encourage each student to use as many types of fruit as he would like. Provide an illustrated recipe card with the following steps on it. Explain the steps to students as you demonstrate the activity. Each student should then follow the recipe.

1. Place 1 spoonful of fruit on your plate.
2. Arrange the fruit in the shape of a rainbow.
3. Repeat steps 1 and 2 until you have a rainbow on your plate.
4. Enjoy your snack!

📖 Library Literature . . . .

The Cloud Book by Tomie de Paola (Holiday House, 1984)
Cloudy With a Chance of Meatballs by Judi Barrett (Aladdin, 1982)
It Looked Like Spilt Milk by Charles G. Shaw (HarperTrophy, 1988)
Rain by Robert Kalan (HarperTrophy, 1991)
Weather Words and What They Mean by Gail Gibbons (Holiday House, 1992)

🎵 Rain Dance . . . .

Supplies: raincoats, rain hats, and boots; tape or CD player; tape or CD of music with rain themes, such as "Singin' in the Rain" performed by Gene Kelly

Setup: Place the supplies on a table in the center.

Directions: Let students put on the rain gear and start the music. Encourage students to dance to the music and pretend they are playing outside during a spring shower.

🍃 ✏️ A Windy Day . . . .

Supplies: lab books; pencils and crayons; plastic drinking straws; 2 muffin tins; large bowl of small objects of varying weights, such as a scrap of paper, coins, blocks, table tennis balls, cotton balls, pieces of cereal, etc.

Setup: Place all of the small objects in the large bowl. Label one muffin tin with the word *Yes* and the other with the word *No*. Place the supplies on a table in the center.

Directions: Have a student select one item from the bowl and place it on the table. Tell her to predict whether the object will move when the "wind" blows. Then, have her blow on the object with a straw. If it moves across the table, she should place it in a section of the muffin tin labeled *Yes*. If it does not move, she should place it in the *No* tin. Have students continue the experiment with all of the items in the bowl. Help them write "Yes" and "No" on two pages of their lab books and draw pictures of the corresponding items.

Weather Cards

Activity found on page 73.

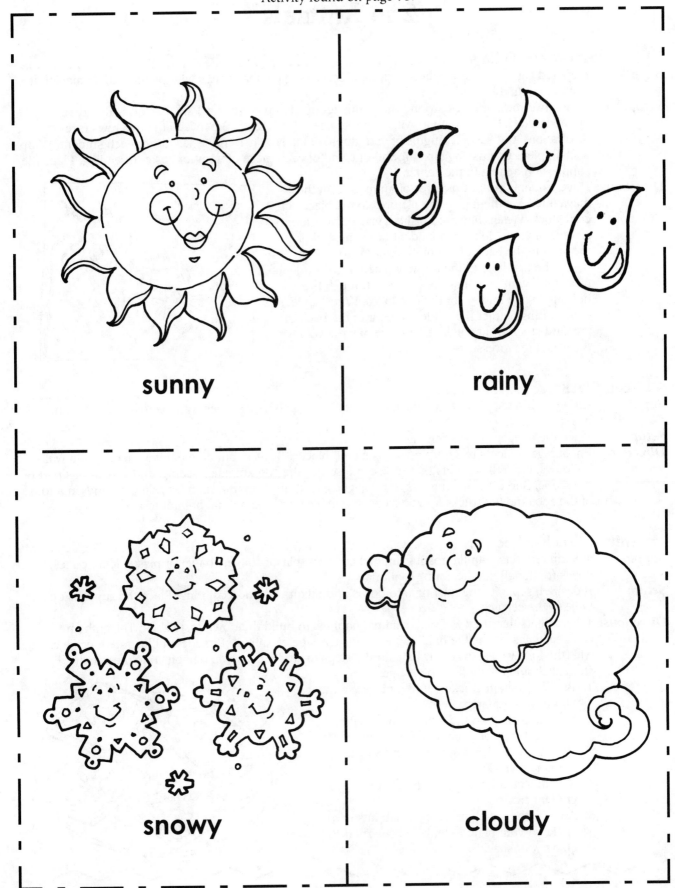

sunny

rainy

snowy

cloudy

Zoo Animals

Framed Zoo Collages

Supplies: prepared card stock or poster board, tape, scissors, glue, magazines with pictures of animals that would be found in a zoo

Setup: Punch two rows of holes around the perimeter of each piece of card stock. Holes should be approximately 2" (5 cm) apart with approximately ½" (1.25 cm) between the two rows (see illustration). Cut several lengths of yarn approximately 2' (61 cm) in length for each student. Wrap a small piece of masking tape around one end of each piece of yarn for easier threading. Place the supplies on a table in the center.

Directions: Have students cut out pictures of animals from the magazines. Let them glue the pictures to the pieces of card stock. When they are finished, give each student a piece of yarn. Help each student tape one end of the yarn to the back of the piece of card stock, just below the first hole in the top row. Then, have students weave the yarn in a crisscross pattern through the holes to create frames for their collages. When a piece of yarn runs out, let the student tape it to the back of the card stock and take another piece of yarn to finish the weaving process.

Zoo Blocks

Supplies: variety of blocks; small zoo animal figurines; small people figurines; vehicle toys, such as a train, a bus, and trucks

Setup: Place the supplies in the center.

Directions: Encourage students to set up a zoo using the blocks. Suggest building habitats, fences and walls, buildings, etc. Tell students that they can also use the zoo animals, people, and vehicles as part of the scene. Suggest using the bus to bring guests into the zoo, the train for riding around on a tour of the zoo, and the trucks for zookeepers to move from one animal habitat to another.

Animal Cracker Zoo

Supplies: graham crackers, vanilla frosting, animal crackers, plastic knives, paper or plastic foam plates, bowls (optional), food coloring (optional)

Setup: If desired, separate the frosting into bowls and mix it with food coloring. Place the supplies on a table in the center.

Directions: Tell students that they will make animal habitats to build their own tasty zoos! The graham crackers will serve as the habitat areas for each type of animal. Provide an illustrated recipe card with the following steps on it. Explain the steps to students as you demonstrate the activity. Each student should then follow the recipe.

1. Break 2 graham crackers into 2 pieces so that you have 4 squares.
2. Spread frosting on the 4 pieces of cracker.
3. Choose 1 type of animal from the animal crackers and stick some of them to 1 piece of graham cracker.
4. Repeat step 3 for the other pieces of graham cracker.
5. Arrange the 4 graham cracker habitats in a circle on your plate to make a zoo. Then, enjoy your snack!

◇ **Library Literature** . . . .
Animals Should Definitely Not Wear Clothing by Judi Barrett (Aladdin, 1988)
Don't Frighten the Lion! by Margaret Wise Brown (HarperCollins Children's Books, 1993)
Good Night, Gorilla by Peggy Rathmann (Putnam Juvenile, 2000)
My Visit to the Zoo by Aliki (HarperTrophy, 1999)
Zoo-Looking by Mem Fox (Scholastic, 1996)

🔢 **Animal Number Match** . . . .
Supplies: prepared Zoo Animal Cards (page 78) in resealable plastic bags
Setup: Make two copies of the Zoo Animal Cards on sturdy card stock. Color and cut apart the cards. On one set of cards, write numbers from 1 to 9. On the other set, draw sets of dots to represent numbers from 1 to 9. Don't write the matching numbers and sets of dots on the same animals. For example, if you write the number 2 on an elephant, draw the two dots on any animal except the other elephant. This will challenge students to match the numbers and dots rather than the types of animals. Laminate the cards for durability. Store each set of cards in a resealable plastic bag. Place the bags on a table in the center.
Directions: Have students remove the cards from the two bags. Tell them to place each set facedown on the table in a grid pattern. Then, let students take turns flipping over two cards, one from each set. If the numbers match, that student keeps the pair and takes another turn. If the numbers do not match, the student turns the two cards facedown and another student takes a turn. The game continues until all of the cards are matched.

♪ **Animal Music** . . . .
Supplies: 8 musical instruments, 5 copies of the Zoo Animal Cards (page 78), enlarged copy of the Musical Staff Pattern (page 16)
Setup: Color and cut apart the animal cards. Laminate the cards and Musical Staff Pattern for durability. Place one set of animal cards in a pile on the table. Use another set to label the instruments by taping a card to each instrument. Attach hook-and-loop tape to the backs of the remaining animal cards and to the front of the Musical Staff Pattern. Hang the Musical Staff Pattern on a wall in the center. Place the animal cards and the instruments on a table.
Directions: Tell students that the animal cards represent musical notes and each animal corresponds to an instrument. Play a few notes to demonstrate. Have students attach the animal cards with hook-and-loop tape to the lines and spaces on the musical staff in any order they wish. Then, tell each student to select a card from the stack on the table to determine which animal instrument she will be playing. Finally, encourage students to play the song by following the notes in the sequence, matching the animals on the musical staff to the animals on the instruments. Suggest that students make the sounds of their animals as they play along.

🍃 **Classifying Zoo Animals** . . . .
Supplies: lab books, pencils and crayons, variety of zoo animals (stuffed, plastic figurines, or laminated pictures), 4 labeled boxes or bins
Setup: Make four signs that say *mammal*, *bird*, *fish*, and *reptile*. Include illustrations of representative animals. Attach each sign to a box. Place the boxes in the center and spread the animals in front of the boxes. Place the other supplies on a table in the center.
Directions: Introduce students to the center by talking about the different kinds of animals that live in a zoo, specifically these four categories and the characteristics that make these groups unique. Have students work together to sort the animals into the four boxes. Let them decide where each animal belongs and why. When the sort is complete, have students draw pictures of the four groups of animals in their lab books.

Zoo Animal Cards

Activities found on page 77.

hippopotamus

lion

bear

elephant

walrus

kangaroo

gorilla

rhinoceros

CD-104198 *It's Center Time!*

Index of Center Activities

Index of Center Activities